USING

COMMON WORSHIP

A Service of
the Word

USING
COMMON WORSHIP
A Service of the Word

A Practical Guide

Tim Stratford

Introduction by Trevor Lloyd

CHURCH HOUSE
PUBLISHING

Church House Publishing
Church House,
Great Smith Street,
London SW1P 3NZ

ISBN   0 7151 2066 2

                Published 2002 by Church House Publishing and *Praxis*

Copyright ©   Praxis *2002*

                All rights reserved. No part of this publication may be reproduced or
                stored or transmitted by any means or in any form, electronic or mechanical,
                including photocopying, recording, or any information storage and retrieval
                system, without written permission which should be sought from the
                Copyright and Contracts Administrator,
                The Archbishops' Council,
                Church House,
                Great Smith Street,
                London SW1P 3NZ.

Telephone   020 7898 1557
Fax   020 7898 1449
Email   *copyright@c-of-e.org.uk*

Cover design
by   Church House Publishing

Printed by   The Cromwell Press Ltd, Trowbridge, Wiltshire

Typeset in   11pt Sabon and 11.5pt Gill Sans
                by Pioneer Associates (Graphic) Ltd, Perthshire

Contents

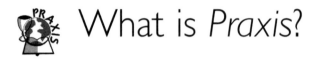 # What is *Praxis*?

Praxis was formed in 1990, sponsored by the Liturgical Commission of the Church of England, the Alcuin Club, and the Group for the Renewal of Worship (GROW). It exists to provide and support liturgical education in the Church of England.

Its aims are:

- to enrich the practice and understanding of worship in the Church of England;

- to serve congregations and clergy in their exploration of the call to worship;

- to provide a forum in which different worshipping traditions can meet and interact.

The name *Praxis* comes from the Greek word for action. It emphasizes our practical concerns and conveys our conviction that worship is a primary expression of the Christian faith.

Praxis runs an annual programme of day conferences and residential workshops around the country, organized either centrally or by *Praxis* regions (informal networks of diocesan liturgical committees).

You can find out more about *Praxis* from our web site: www.sarum.ac.uk/praxis/

For a copy of the *Praxis* programme and details of how to affiliate, contact the *Praxis* office:

Praxis
St Matthew's House
20 Great Peter Street
LONDON
SWIP 2BU
Tel: 020 7222 3704
Fax: 020 7233 0255
Email: praxis@London.com

Foreword to the series

Those who produced the *Common Worship* services wanted to
provide liturgical resources that encourage worshipping
communities to take account of the pastoral needs of the
congregation and the mission imperative of worship that engages
with the surrounding culture.

The synodical process has, rightly, focused on the texts, the
structures and the rubrics. But the services will only come to life
and reach their potential as living encounters with God in the
nitty-gritty of worship in parish churches, hospital and prison
chapels, school halls and other centres of worship. *Praxis* was set
up by the Liturgical Commission in partnership with The Group
for the Renewal of Worship (GROW) and the Alcuin Club to
foster just such a practical approach to liturgy – working at grass
roots level to support real churches who are seeking to make
their regular worship better. *Praxis* has been running training
events and courses to this end for ten years and it is a great step
forward to see the combination of deeper understanding and
better practice coming together in print.

The *Using Common Worship* series is a creative partnership
between *Praxis* and Church House Publishing which will help all
of us to make the most of *Common Worship*. Each volume
bridges the gap between the bare texts and the experience of
using those texts in worship. Full of practical advice, backed up
with the underlying thinking from members of the Liturgical
Commission, these books will be a valuable tool to put alongside
the *Common Worship* volumes on the shelves of every worship
leader in the Church of England.

✠ *David Sarum*
Chairman of the Liturgical Commission

Acknowledgements

My thanks are warmly offered to members of the Church of the Good Shepherd, West Derby in Liverpool for allowing me the space to write these pages and for being enthusiastic about trying out new ways of worship and allowing imagination some exercise. Without this I would have had very little basis for writing anything at all.

Thanks also to members of GROW and to those friends and colleagues in *Praxis* and *Praxis* North West who create the space in which worship can be explored, through which I have learnt so much.

Thanks especially to those who have helped with the text: to Jen, my wife, and her mum, Elaine Stanley, who have made what I have written more readable and user friendly; to Mark Earey and Kathryn Pritchard for the original idea of this book, their technical assistance and encouragement.

Copyright acknowledgements

Introduction
Trevor Lloyd

What is A Service of the Word?

A Service of the Word (ASOTW) is an unusual service for the Church of England. It looks very short, takes up only one page, and yet is capable of almost infinite expansion. It could take five minutes, or be the framework for a whole day of worship. This is possible because it consists entirely of rubrics or instructions, together with a couple of pages of notes. Together these describe the structure of the service, and its essential and optional elements.

Where did this apparently not very Anglican concept come from? In June 1986 David Silk, then Archdeacon of Leicester, and I took to the House of Bishops a paper from the Liturgical Commission, which we had drafted, entitled 'The scope for liturgical work 1986–1991'. It was the usual practice for the Commission to take to the Bishops an outline of what we had in mind, so that the House of Bishops, as the body responsible for introducing liturgical business into the Church of England General Synod, could agree to the work being done. But the idea we took was unusual, if not slightly revolutionary. It was for a Church of England 'Directory of Worship'.

We had outlined some aims:

1. To provide some indication of different ways of doing liturgy, taking into account sociological, architectural and churchmanship differences.

2. To indicate where advantage might be taken of notes and rubrics in *The Alternative Service Book 1980*, to develop and enrich the liturgy.

3. To provide outline structures and mandatory sections for

some main services, which . . . would provide greater freedom for those who wish either to enrich or to shorten the services (including 'Family' services and worship in Urban Priority Areas).

We pointed out that the Commission had already gained some experience in producing 'coaching hints' for those preparing services, as well as a range of resource material, in compiling *Lent, Holy Week, Easter*. In that book, two years earlier, we had already trailed the directory concept in the Chairman's introduction: 'We are providing a *directory* from which choices may be made. We think of this book as a manual to be used with selectivity, sensitivity and imagination.' The book contained, for instance, two pages on the Agape (Greek for love, used for the 'love-feast' on Maundy Thursday). This gave some description of the background and possible approaches to the service, followed by an outline Holy Communion order based on Rite A interspersed with rubrics such as 'The main course of a simple meal may be taken here.' – one of the forerunners of the outline approach followed in A Service of the Word.

We outlined how the needs of those working in Urban Priority Areas (highlighted in the *Faith in the City* report) and those producing 'Family' services might be met by the directory 'structure-plus-resource' approach, and suggested that a number of structures might be provided by the Commission, including one for Rite A Holy Communion.

But perhaps the most far-reaching suggestion was one that might result in saving a great deal of Synod's time spent in agreeing the details of texts. If there could be agreement about the basic structure of different services, then Synod could decide which texts had to be mandatory 'in order to secure doctrinal orthodoxy and to avoid the divisions which would be caused by "party" texts.' In the communion service, for example, 'there could be mandatory texts only for those things which have been carefully worked over by Synod in order to secure doctrinal agreement: the prayer for the dead paragraph in the intercessions, the form of absolution, the anamnesis [remembrance] sections in the eucharistic prayers. There might be advantages in encouraging creative innovation in the thanksgiving section and the acclamations of eucharistic prayers. We would need only permission to invent or extemporise further proper prefaces . . .'

Though the Bishops at the time agreed that this was a suitable programme of work for the Commission to embark on, subsequent meetings of the House of Bishops, when the completed proposals were presented in the draft edition of *Patterns for Worship* in 1989, regarded some of these suggestions, particularly about the communion service, as far too revolutionary. At that point, as the Introduction to *New Patterns for Worship* says,

> The House of Bishops said it was 'mindful of those who want a period of stability in the liturgical life of the Church, and who might be anxious lest the Commission's proposals extend the bounds of choice and variety of liturgical provision more widely than has been customary in the Church of England'.
>
> The 1995 edition established the principle followed in *Common Worship* of publishing both commended and authorized material in one volume. It included the new authorized Service of the Word, Confessions and Absolutions and Affirmations of Faith, but the eucharistic proposals were omitted.

There were three things that made these proposals seem a little revolutionary, and each of them had been the subject of considerable and reasoned historical and liturgical discussion on the Commission.

Authority

First, there were some interlocking issues around the theme of authority. Historically there are two ways in which a liturgical and reformed church can maintain doctrinal integrity and discipline. The one traditionally favoured by the Church of England is to make the liturgy the touchstone of doctrinal authority: if you want to know what the Church believes, look at its liturgy. That is why ministers, at their ordination and on taking up subsequent appointments, promise in their Declaration of Assent (*Common Worship: Services and Prayers for the Church of England*, page xi) that 'in public prayer and administration of the sacraments, I will use only the forms of service which are authorized or allowed by Canon.' This is one way, in formal terms, of guaranteeing to congregations that they have a minister who will not lead them astray doctrinally. It is also the reason why the *Book of Common Prayer* is enshrined in the 1974 Worship and Doctrine Measure, with the General Synod undertaking 'to ensure the forms of service contained in the *Book of Common Prayer* continue to be available for use in the Church of England' and that any new forms of service are 'neither contrary to, nor indicative of any departure from, the doctrine of the Church of England in any essential matter.' Significantly, the Measure says where the doctrine of the Church of England may be found: 'such doctrine is to be found in the Thirty-Nine Articles of Religion, the *Book of Common Prayer* and the Ordinal.' This is set out on page 52 of *New Patterns*. The traditional Anglican adherence to the view that it is the form of words in the liturgy, and not simply a formal doctrinal statement, which sets the standard of doctrine is also the reason why successive Lambeth Conferences have set such store by the *Book of Common Prayer* as the unifying factor of the Anglican Communion, long after that Book had ceased to be used and had rightly been replaced by more local forms.

The other way to maintain doctrinal integrity is to have a doctrinal statement to which everyone subscribes. This was the pattern in the continental reformed churches, which produced confessions of faith usually far longer than the Thirty-Nine Articles. It happened in England in the seventeenth century. The Westminster Assembly, appointed by Parliament to reform the Church of England in 1643, had as its initial task the revision of the Thirty-Nine Articles, and produced *The Westminster Confession* – thirty-three chapters covering nearly fifty pages – which was eventually approved by Parliament in 1648. As well as compiling the Larger and the Shorter Catechisms, it also produced, in 1645, *The Directory for the Publick Worship of God*. Instead of a liturgy, this contained directions and instructions, sets of rubrics with some sample prayers, telling the minister to pray 'to this or the like effect', the forerunner of that ASB phrase 'in these or similar words'. In a church where those who led the worship were bound by a heavyweight doctrinal statement, the liturgy could be handled in a lighter and less prescriptive or legalistic way.

In listing the sources of Church of England doctrine as a set of historical documents – the Articles, the *Book of Common Prayer* and the Ordinal – and requiring everyone to accept that if the General Synod approved something then it must be in conformity with that historic deposit, the 1974 Worship and Doctrine Measure lifted from any new liturgical forms the burden of carrying the full weight of conveying and embodying the doctrine of the Church. Whether or not this will prove to have been a wise or spiritually helpful move will only be known in a century or so, but the effect on those compiling and planning worship in the early twenty-first century is that – quite legally – we enjoy far more freedom and variety in our worship than at any time in the history of the English Church. Part of the mechanism for conveying that freedom has been the structure of A Service of the Word, together with the publication of the original *Patterns for Worship*. It is not insignificant that the working title for *Patterns*, to within a year of its publication, was 'The Directory.'

The Word Service

The second area of debate in the Liturgical Commission was the structure and content of the 'Word Service' and its relationship to the Eucharist. Some of the reasoning behind this debate can still be seen in the current edition, in 'Service Structures: some historical background' in the chapter on Planning and Preparation. The debate, parallel with that on the nature of the Daily Office, took us back both to Jewish patterns of prayer and to early Christian patterns such as that of Justin Martyr, writing in the mid second century:

And on the day called Sun-day an assembly is held in one place of all who live in town or country, and the records of all the apostles or writings of the prophets are read for as long as time allows.

Then, when the reading has finished the president in a discourse admonishes and exhorts us to imitate these good things.

Then we all stand up together and offer prayers.

When we have ended the prayers, we greet one another with a kiss. Then bread and a cup of water and of mixed wine are brought to him who presides . . . and he takes them and offers praise and glory to the Father of all in the name of the Son and of the Holy Spirit, and gives thanks at some length.

The introduction to the first edition of *Patterns* drew three conclusions from history:

First, a clear structure is essential. Its main components should stand out so that worshippers can see the shape, development and climax of the service – so that they 'know where they are going'.

Second, 'word services' of different structures should be regarded as an interchangeable first part of Holy Communion.

Third, as we see the three different types of service come together in history, and as it is fairly unlikely that a parish would have three different types of 'word service' each Sunday, we need a balance in any one service, between prayer and praise, word and teaching. This means we should not have a service which is nothing but teaching, without praise and prayer; nor a service which is nothing but praise, without some word and teaching.

One significant step forward was our discussion about how far it was possible to reduce the service of morning or evening prayer to a rubric about its basic elements. That was when we came up with 'The service shall consist of Word, Prayer, Praise and Action.' Put in a beginning and an ending, and there it is. The fact that A Service of the Word now consists of a page rather than one line is the result of two bits of further reflection, both in the Commission and in the subsequent Synod process. First, though in theory these items could come just once or many times, and might vary in order, it would be helpful to indicate a normative order, with permissions for variation. Second, returning to the question, 'Are there matters here where the whole Church should be saying the same thing, or using only an agreed number of texts?' led to one or two sensitive items – Confession and Absolution, and Affirmation of Faith for instance – being restricted to authorized texts.

'Word, Prayer, Praise and Action' remains as the basic explanation in the introductory material in *New Patterns for Worship* (page 15), though with more careful explanation about the nature of the different elements and the way they relate to one another. Action, for instance, is not something that usually happens on its own, but may happen in combination with one of the other elements. In some ways it is unhelpful that these are not the main headings of the sections of the service; rather they are ingredients which may come more than once. *New Patterns* uses the 'television chef' kind of approach, by describing the sections (Preparation, Liturgy of the Word, Prayers) as three tubs into which you put these ingredients.

> It is a bit like preparing a meal with three courses, plus an appetizer at the beginning and coffee at the end. Each course has a number of different ingredients, which can be used more than once in different combinations in different courses.

No doubt others involved in educating people to use this service will invent other ways of describing what to do. Builders, for instance, may wish to discard the liturgical cook-book in favour of computer-assisted design. Here is the entrance hall to your bungalow, where you greet your host, say hullo and recognize who else is at the party, before going into the kitchen/dining room for food and nourishment. Tempted to close your eyes immediately after a good meal, you are ushered into the lounge for party games or discussion, applying the energy and insight just received to life, and praising the skills of your host. There are bedrooms, for closing your eyes, resting in God's presence, meditating and praying, before you find the back door, saying goodbye and thinking about what you take with you – energy for tomorrow, the concern of friends, more to pray about. Air stewards or stewardesses may think of take-off and landing as the beginning and ending, with all that happens in between, the serving of newspapers (relevant liturgy, this), pre-packaged plastic food, the joyful recognition of old films, and the desperation of confession, prayer and faith on a turbulent day.

Common prayer

The third major area of debate was about the nature of common prayer and the question 'What is it that makes our worship recognizably Anglican?' This is an exercise to try with any Church of England congregation. Ask what the basic elements are that make up an Anglican service. When I was a curate, I used to ask this in our church school, and children often started their list with 'the collection'. This does not necessarily mean that we made it the most important part of the service, simply that the children remembered because it was an action bit of the worship which involved them personally. The initial answers the Commission gave to this question are summed up in the Discussion Starter on Common Prayer in *New Patterns*:

> We believe that some of the marks which should be safeguarded for those who wish to stand in any recognizable continuity with historic Anglican tradition are:
>
> - a recognizable structure for worship;
> - an emphasis on reading the word and on using psalms;
> - liturgical words repeated by the congregation, some of which, like the creed, would be known by heart;
> - using a collect, the Lord's Prayer, and some responsive forms in prayer;
> - a recognition of the centrality of the Eucharist;
> - a concern for form, dignity, and economy of words.

In the Liturgical Commission's 1993 book *The Renewal of Common Prayer* the concept of common prayer was summed up as consisting in structures that are clear and known, and some texts that are familiar and some of which may be known by heart. It is the combination of structure and texts which holds together the family of liturgies across the Anglican Communion, and which creates a recognizable family likeness between, for instance, 'family' services in different parts of England.

This approach is not absolutely novel. The 1872 Act of Uniformity Amendment Act, as well as permitting a shortened form of Morning and Evening Prayer, allowed for a 'third service' to be composed entirely from the familiar words of the Scriptures and the *Book of Common Prayer*. That was one way of answering the question 'Which texts?'

But the Liturgical Commission saw the texts that held the Church together as made up of two types. First, there were authorized texts, in response to the question 'What are those areas about which there might be controversy or division, where the Church should be seen to unite around one text, or one group of texts, which have been debated by General Synod and therefore cannot be seen as "party" texts?' The answer to this question can be seen in A Service of the Word in the use of the word 'authorized' before Prayers of Penitence, Creed and Affirmation of Faith. In A Service of the Word with Holy Communion, a Collect and the Eucharistic Prayer must also follow an authorized text. The second type of text is the memorable, familiar material including prayers, psalms, songs and hymns, which varies from church to church, but in which there is probably a common core of well-known material.

The Result

A Service of the Word is the result of the coming together of these three strands of historical and liturgical discussion, about questions of authority, the nature of the Word Service, and the nature of common prayer. But its production and use was in no sense a remote theological and academic exercise. The initial motivation came from the down-to-earth requests about worship in the *Faith in the City* report and from the continuing requests for forms of service that were really suitable for all ages. It is one of the few elements in *Common Worship* which was tested extensively in inner urban areas and which had some years of authorized use before its final revision for that book. One significant change at its last revision in 1998 was the inclusion of a parallel outline form for use with Holy Communion. This not only provides a slightly greater degree of freedom in the communion service, but also enables churches to have the same pattern of worship week by week, sometimes going on to communion and sometimes not, usually depending on the availability of an ordained president. In doing so, it safeguards the unity of the sacrament while acknowledging clearly its two component parts of word and communion.

It would be a mistake to see A Service of the Word as especially designed for those whose normal diet is a word-based all-age service. It is equally helpful for those who are the heirs to the Parish Communion movement, and may even be a factor in bringing together these two different traditions in a way that meets the needs of the worshipping Church in the twenty-first century.

Over the last twenty years we have seen the Church of England move towards the position where A Service of the Word is now established as part of *Common Worship*, bringing with it a new freedom and great possibilities for different styles of worship. Together with the range of resources represented in *New Patterns for Worship* this both opens up an exciting vista for those who plan worship in the local church and also lays on them a responsibility to ensure that they do it well. This book is designed to help those who use A Service of the Word to do so with at least as much vision, imagination and liturgical understanding as that with which it was designed.

Note: As in *New Patterns for Worship*, 2nd edn, 2002, throughout this book references simply to *Common Worship* (CW) refer to the main *Common Worship* volume, *Common Worship: Services and Prayers for the Church of England*. The other *Common Worship* volumes are referred to by their full titles, for example *Common Worship: Pastoral Services*.

1 | The directory approach

If you are sitting down with a blank piece of paper and the responsibility for giving order and shape to an act of worship that is looming large and doesn't fit in with the regular pattern, then this book is for you. But I hope its use will extend beyond that. A Service of the Word (ASOTW) opens up a range of exciting possibilities that we will explore in the following chapters: ideas that can be used from time to time or all year round; ways of working that can tap the creativity of wider circles of people; and a discussion of the principles that underlie the Church's thinking about worship.

Chiefly this book aims to open up the possibilities that ASOTW can offer to the worship, ministry and mission of the Church of England. The flexibility of structure and content that it encourages can be used imaginatively and creatively to make worship come alive and connect with countless moments in the life of a community, without cutting loose from the moorings of the Church of England. *New Patterns for Worship* will be a key resource for this, but we will draw on the whole Common Worship collection and much from the world Church beyond it. The range is perplexing and the security of the familiar can seem like an attractive refuge. There are times when safety should be sought but there are times when the boat should be pushed out. Here is some encouragement and guidance for doing so.

In this chapter we shall look at how to make the most of all this. Later chapters consider the use of ASOTW for All-Age Worship; as a form of Morning or Evening Prayer; in a eucharistic setting; and finally with particular groups or for one-off and special occasions. The last chapter opens up some discussion about the new skills that churches will need to foster in order to use this effectively.

The use of ASOTW is potentially very broad indeed and this author has worked only in a limited number of contexts. For this reason what follows is not exhaustive but merely illustrative. It is intended to inspire and not to limit. Where dos and don'ts are mentioned it is fully recognized that these may have seemed important because of the author's particular context. Nevertheless, they will perhaps serve to alert readers to potential problems, although some readers will have been ahead of the author in seeing their way through to better solutions.

Context

The 'directory approach' begins with the assumption that the 'best' sort of worship is sensitive to the context in which it takes place and for which it is designed. Context is always particular. No two gatherings are the same. There may be strong common strands, but the Church is at its strongest when it can truly relate to the here and now in each locality. The context for any given service of worship will be affected by factors such as:

- its purpose (evangelistic, missionary, or pastoral);

- the age range of those who will be present;

- the nature of a geographic locality, which may have a cultural distinctiveness and different codes of speech to those that dominate the Church;

- the season or moment, be it Christmas or a 200th anniversary, death, disaster or celebration;

- the space in which the meeting takes place; and that may not always be a church building. Worship in the high street or a school assembly hall shouldn't just be a replica of what would be done on a Sunday morning in a church.

In simple terms, what is needed is some sensitivity to the time and place, concerns, hopes and dreams of those who gather.

So, when putting together ASOTW, make sure you consider:

- the pastoral context;

- your limitations;

- the church building for which it is being designed;

- the expectations of those who will come to worship.

In effect ASOTW passes on the responsibility for meeting these needs from a central church authority to those who are closer to the local and particular situation. The very purpose of ASOTW is to harness the benefits of this. So allow for innovation and exploration in worship in order to try and meet a community's needs and aspirations. But remember that it comes with some responsibility. More of this will be discussed later.

Although ASOTW is relatively new to the Church as a formal provision, the creation of local services has gone on for longer. Indeed, ASOTW is partly a response by the Church of England to practice that has been ahead of the legal framework. For instance, there has never been any official provision for 'Family Services'. Most churches simply developed their own forms for these more informal services, or used material from sources such as the Church Pastoral Aid Society. This means that many parishes have forms of service in place, either of their own drafting or from pre-published sources, that predate ASOTW. Now is the time to look afresh at these forms of service with the new insights offered in A Service of the Word and *New Patterns for Worship*. Now that the Church of England can recognize and affirm locally produced material, perhaps this is also the right time to check whether the material you use conforms to the wider Church's sense of good practice.

A Service of the Word and *New Patterns*

Although ASOTW has been around for some time and is the basis of much of the Church of England's new liturgy (including Morning and Evening Prayer), it is when it is used alongside *New Patterns for Worship* that it comes into its own.

There are three main sections to *New Patterns for Worship* after its Introduction. These are:

- Commentary

- Resources

- Sample services.

A Service of the Word is formally printed out in the Introduction, to provide the basis for the use of all that follows.[1] ASOTW itself, and its accompanying introduction and notes, combines enormous scope in most aspects of the service with some limitations in others. The limitations are few, and are intended to help worship leaders avoid the worst pitfalls and retain some moorings to the Church of England.

The Resources Section

In the Resources Section you will find a large collection of liturgical ideas, prayers and responses organized according to the way in which they might be used in a service. So there are subsections for 'Gathering and Greeting', 'Penitence', 'Liturgy of the Word', 'Psalms & Canticles', 'Affirmations of Faith', 'Prayers', 'Praise', 'Peace', 'Action and Movement' and 'Conclusion'. Every section begins with a story from each of four imaginary churches, St Ann's, St Bartholomew's, St Christopher's and St Dodo's, together with a few dos and don'ts. This is followed by a substantial body of resource material – a smorgasbord from which you can take whatever morsels suit your needs. To help your eye see what's what more easily there is a sub-heading at the beginning of each item that offers a clue to its focus.

According to Canon Law, there are some elements of worship in the Church of England that must only be drawn from properly authorized sources. In the context of ASTOW this means only:

- the Prayers of Penitence; and

- the Affirmation of Faith.

The sections in *New Patterns for Worship* which cover these elements bring together *all* the authorized texts from the various parts of CW so that they are easy to find. If it's authorized it's there: if it isn't there it isn't authorized.

All of this means that there is considerable freedom to look well beyond the Church's official provision for inspiration and even to write your own material for much of the service. But beware! Not every freedom given must always be used in every place and at every time.

(If the service includes Holy Communion there must also be other authorized material, which is *not* included in *New Patterns for Worship*: a Collect and a Eucharistic Prayer.)

Commentary Section

The Commentary Section offers the sort of good advice that is always a helpful and necessary reminder. In churches where there is a worship group or committee that helps plan services, or offers reflection and evaluation, this section could even be used as curriculum and study material for their education and training.

Sample Services Section

The Standard Samples offer good starting points for turning the resources into something that helps people to worship. Although some of them can simply be photocopied and used straightforwardly, they are best regarded as templates to trigger the imagination. Under no circumstances should you consider buying a copy of *New Patterns* for every member of the congregation as a means of using these samples regularly. The book is not designed for congregational use but is primarily a resource book. The samples, however, can be printed locally and some could be made available for purchase on individual cards. Undoubtedly the range of such services emerging from both official and unofficial sources will grow as time rolls on. The samples provided in the book include three 'Word Services', four 'Communion Services', five 'Seasonal Services' and six services for 'Specials'. In addition, there are several service 'outlines' that show how services (or worship within small group meetings) might be structured and the sort of resources that might be used.

It is possible to slip *New Patterns for Worship*'s resource material into A Service of the Word or a Communion service without ever looking at the other sections. However, you will get much more from *New Patterns* if you set aside time to sit down and read the Introduction and Commentary. When you are putting a service together, look at the stories ahead of each resource subsection as you dip into it, to be sure you avoid the common pitfalls they describe.

Starting to plan a service

As noted earlier, the starting point for working with A Service of the Word must always be to consider the context for which you are preparing. The questions below can be used to help:

- What is the age range of those for whom the service is being prepared?

- Is there a particular pastoral context to the gathering, e.g. an anniversary or celebration?

- What brings people together? Do they share a common concern through their work, condition or life-style?

- What else might be part of the shared journey or expectations of the groups for whom worship is being prepared?

- What skills and gifts might those who are coming to worship have to bring?

- What is the time of year or season? For what day of the week and for what time is this worship being prepared?

- What is the nature of the building and facilities that will be available?

- What might God be saying here?

ASOTW may well be used for some of the regular Sunday worship of the church and many of the assumptions normally made for these occasions can be relied upon. But even so it is important to ask, 'What is it that makes ASOTW particularly appropriate in place of anything else?'

Whether you are sitting down with a blank piece of paper or adapting a service, the next thing to do is decide on the aim of the event for which you are planning. Even if you are using familiar forms of service, standard patterns or published services (such as the Sample Services from *New Patterns for Worship*), always be clear about your aims for the particular act of worship you are planning. The aim for a service might include deciding on a governing 'theme' – though it is important to note that aim and theme are not the same thing. If you focus on a theme alone, you risk turning an act of worship into simply a time of learning. The aim of the service will be much broader and will include an element of *dynamic* – 'Where is this service going?', 'What is it doing?', etc. A Service of the Word is not simply an excuse to pull together some favourite bits of worship material but a way of meeting particular pastoral, missionary or local concerns through the liturgy and bringing them into the worship of the church.

Finding a 'theme' with the Common Worship lectionary

The three-year *Common Worship* Sunday lectionary does not provide ready-made 'themes' in the way that the ASB lectionary did. Not only is there not a list of themes equivalent to ASB page 1092[2] but it would be quite impossible to draw up such a list because the CW lectionary doesn't work in the same way. The CW lectionary is based on a fundamental distinction between parts of the year that are strongly 'seasonal' and parts of the year that are 'ordinary', without a strong seasonal flavour.

The 'seasonal time' consists basically of the incarnational cycle (from 1 November to 2 February) and the Easter cycle (Ash Wednesday to Pentecost Sunday). In these parts of the year the readings, collects and additional seasonal material are all aligned with the thrust of the season. This gives a fairly clear sense of a 'seasonal theme', even though it does not assign particular themes to particular Sundays. (See pages 91–5 for further implications of the seasons and the choice of readings.)

During the periods of Ordinary Time between these two strong seasonal cycles there is neither a seasonal flavour nor a particular Sunday theme:

- The focus of the Collect of the day is not necessarily connected to the Post Communion Collect or the readings. (The Collect of the day stands in its own right as a prayer through which worshippers can invite God to continue the work of salvation in and through them. The Post Communion Collect reflects primarily on the way that the Eucharist can bring about change in the worshipping community.)

- The readings themselves are not necessarily related to each other but are largely selected to encourage a semi-continuous reading through books of the Old Testament and New Testament as well as the Gospels. (For some Sundays there is a 'related' track that offers a Psalm and an Old Testament reading that will bear some relation to the Gospel – but even here, it is not always easy to discern related themes.)

This leaves the door wide open for you to work out the thrust or theme for a service you are planning, depending on what you choose to make the focus.

This openness is just what is needed. People no longer share so many common concerns, and a set of all-embracing themes worked out 20 years ago seem irrelevant today. You will find yourself pushed to rely not on centrally produced wisdom but on asking where God is leading you here and now, and then looking for what will help to express that in worship.

There is a further alternative for the period of Ordinary Time. The CW lectionary allows for other patterns of Bible readings to be determined locally and used outside the seasonal periods of the year. *New Patterns* provides over forty such patterns of readings, but others can be devised by the local church or may be provided by other organizations. Such patterns of readings might cover particular books of the Bible, or biblical characters, or themes. Where these are used, then the theme has effectively chosen the Bible readings, rather than the readings providing the basis for a theme.

Of course, ASOTW is not restricted to Sunday use. Outside the regular occasions for worship there is much less guidance about what readings should be used.

On choosing a theme

Care should be taken to ensure that there is some overall direction, some sense of cohesion, of going somewhere, some development in the congregation's relationship to God, reflected in the service structure. Sometimes this is provided by a clear theme. The theme may be determined by the occasion or season, such as Mothering Sunday or Christmas, or by some local event, such as a patronal festival or jazz festival. The theme will also be regularly determined by the Bible readings. Sometimes no clear overall theme will emerge, and the Bible reading, prayers and praise will be left, like coloured glass in a kaleidoscope, to cast light on one another and to provide, in the interplay of patterns, different pictures for different people in the congregation. The important thing is to recognize which of these routes is being followed. Ask the question, either on your own or in a planning group, 'What do we expect to happen to people in this service? What will be the outcomes in terms of Christian growth, education, deepening appreciation of God, experience of him in worship and praise, and in obedience to his word?' And that outcome, and the development through the service, will be partly determined by giving some attention to the emotional flow of the service. Does it start quietly and build up, start on a 'high' and become reflective, or have a climax in the middle?

New Patterns for Worship, pages 15–16

Putting it all together

It is not possible to provide a list of rules to follow for the next steps after deciding on the aim, in order to create the perfect Service of the Word. It is difficult to tie down the creative process to a particular single recipe. *New Patterns* offers Sample Structures, complete Sample Services and pages of resources that can be drawn upon, amended and adapted as needed. Add to this a good knowledge of the local situation, along with imagination, ideas picked up from other resource books, people and places, all with a good dose of prayerful reflection.

Beyond *New Patterns*

There was a time when the only choices that local churches had to make about worship were limited to choosing hymns. In A Service of the Word the shape and content of almost every element involves choices, and those choices extend well beyond the Church of England's officially published material (with the exception of Affirmations of Faith, Prayers of Penitence and, for Eucharists, the Collects and Eucharistic Prayers).

Those who use ASOTW are invited to create new symbolic actions, turn to alternative liturgical and poetic words, innovate with movement and shape, and so on.

There are a lot of good ideas that have already been tried and tested. Often the best ideas are found when your own spirit is touched during worship prepared by somebody else. If prayer, poetry, dance, drama, or music has helped you worship or a sense of structure and journey in the liturgy has carried you along, then they could do so for others too. Don't be reluctant to build on the innovations of others where it helps. This is how the Church itself grows and develops.

Where people earn their livelihoods through developing such resources, be careful about simply borrowing them without the appropriate permission and royalties.[3] Where this isn't so, you are often free to borrow the idea and develop it in your own way, and the original innovators may well be pleased when this happens.

There are also many published sources to be found in books, church newspapers, magazines and on websites. Don't restrict yourself simply to the liturgy shelves of a bookshop. Good material for use with children can often be found in the children's section. Devotional books, spirituality books and daily patterns of readings can be helpful quarries. Don't ignore the shelves of Church history – much original source material can be found there. And remember that it isn't the case that hymns are sung and everything else is said – look at musical settings for responses, thanksgivings, creeds, canticles (such as the Gloria, etc.), which are available in a wide range of styles.

See Appendix 1 for some recommended resources that represent a variety of styles.

So, among the keys to using ASOTW are:

- recognizing the determining features of the occasion you are preparing for;
- finding the resources you need from *New Patterns*, your own creative energy and other sources accessible to you.

We will now move on to consider some particular ways in which ASOTW can be used.

2 All-age worship

In the parish setting A Service of the Word is most likely to be advertised as All-Age Worship. This is probably because it owes its existence to the forms of 'family service' that started to emerge half a century ahead of the Church of England authorizing this provision. Whilst the phrase 'A Service of the Word' is a useful handle in the Common Worship books, it is not as helpfully accessible as words like 'Family Service'. This means that it is not a very good name to use as a signpost for people to decide which worship is appropriate for them. For a service that may be quite interactive and full of action, drama and symbol, it seems quite inappropriate to describe it principally as 'of the Word'.

Titles can, and should, help describe your worship and even convey some of its underlying principles. So-called 'family services' emerged in an age when the nuclear family was increasingly prominent as a Christian ideal, whilst at the same time it was felt to be under threat in Western society. They offered the opportunity to affirm this ideal and to encourage the Church to regard itself as a great family in which Jesus was a brother and his father our Father.

All-age worship is not a family service by another name. The underlying philosophy is quite different and this belongs to another moment in history. At the beginning of the third millennium there is a greater awareness within the Church that God blesses society in many ways. This may be through the extended family or through other forms of domestic arrangement that inevitably create the warp and weft of many communities. There is also a greater awareness of the pain felt by some of those who live alone, through no choice of their own, either because of lack of opportunity, death or abandonment. And society is more aware of those who have found their own nuclear family a place of abuse or exclusion. Whilst family life can offer the very best of love, commitment and security, there are people who come to church for whom this may or may not be true. These people may be of all ages, including the very aged and the very young. All-age worship is not about letting go of an ideal but about creating the environment for worship through which everybody can feel included.

> *What is all-age worship?*
>
> - **Worship**: this is not simply an opportunity for teaching nor simply a fun event for a wide age range. Worship is a spiritual activity through which people should be able to hold their deepest concerns and greatest hopes before God and in which they can allow God to form them. In worship people express and declare God's worth, praising him for who he is and what he does.
>
> - **All-age**: it is not just for children. But the history of Christian worship bears much more relation to the concerns of adults than children, so the distinctiveness of all-age worship is that children are included.

In this chapter we will focus mainly on what is often a problem in local churches: how to integrate children into worship and the worshipping community.

Making it worship

There is no prescribed formula to guarantee that an event is worship. Whether or not somebody who goes to church manages to worship God can depend partly on the externals that the church provides, e.g. hospitality, liturgy, music, symbol; it also depends partly on the person's own preparedness, mood, stress and distress and on intangibles such as atmosphere, awe and a sense of God's presence. These things matter for every age of worshipper.

Worship in itself is not confined to one mood. People gather for worship on both Good Friday and Easter Day, for funerals and for weddings, in gladness and in pain. The cross is held before the worshipping community as much as the resurrection. It is not necessarily the goal of worship that people should leave feeling on top of the world with their egos nicely massaged. But it should be a goal for worship that people are drawn into an encounter with the living God to whom they can relate as a heavenly Father, whose love is both spurned and yet needed by humanity.

The next thing to remember is that worship is not a teaching session but a way in which we can let God shape us. In jargon: it is not 'educational' but it should be 'formational'. In all-age worship this boundary often gets confused. The Church is involved in people's training, education and formation. All three relate to worship in different ways but really ought to be distinguished. The fundamental concern of worship is to provide the space for Christian people to encounter the God who 'breaks, melts, moulds and fills' them.

- **Training**: here the primary concern is learning a skill (how to do something). In relation to worship this might mean reading, leading intercessions, singing, acting, dancing, preaching, etc. Whilst the worshipping community needs to be tolerant of those who are developing their skills in these ways, training is not a key function of worship. People will need to practise in actual times of worship and should receive some evaluation from real worshippers. For the sake of the worshipping community, however, they should also be given some training outside worship – for preaching as well as dancing.

- **Education**: the Church's role as an educator is born out of its concern for people to be equipped in the best possible way to make sense of the world they live in and to engage with others in interpreting it. In relation to worship this might mean understanding why the Church does what it does. An understanding of communion may be discussed at a confirmation group or in children's First Communion preparation. As Christian people grow, their understanding of the Church's worship should continue to be extended, drawing on the fields of anthropology, history, biblical studies, linguistics, etc. and pitched at helping mature Christian adults understand themselves. Sometimes it may be appropriate to use the sermon slot for this sort of learning. More often it will be appropriate to offer learning opportunities outside of worship. Many dioceses offer a module on worship as part of an accredited course.

- **Formation**: it is God who forms the people of God. The role of the Church's worship in relation to Christian formation is to create an environment in which people can open themselves to God's shaping hand. This happens in the encounter with the divine and also in an encounter with each other. Through the words of the liturgy, hymnody and the Bible, through shared reflection and intercession, by commitment and decision and testimony, God moves his people on. Worship needs to be planned with this in mind and with an understanding of the formational needs of every age group.

Whilst training and education can relate to worship, worship should primarily be geared to formation.

The right sort of aim

All-age worship presents the greatest temptation to slip from formation into education. One of the earliest tasks in the planning of worship is to decide on an aim, but don't make this an educational aim too often. The ASB tended to encourage this by offering ready-made themes, like a sort of curriculum for understanding God and 'Salvation History'. The themes were then worked out through sentences, collects, prefaces and blessings, which all served to throw light on the lectionary readings and consequent sermon. This can make the liturgy little more than a helpful context for teaching. As described in the previous chapter, those who try to use Common Worship in this way will find it unhelpful because it doesn't follow the same rules.

The liturgy should not be understood as the context for a teaching syllabus dictated by the lectionary. Other important factors should be considered when deciding on an aim (see the list on page 16 for examples). So, for instance, an all-age service for the Sunday before Christmas is bound to be controlled by the season, but it can do more than simply teach the Incarnation (see the panel for an alternative).

The Christmas theme and a Christmas aim

- An **educational** concern to describe both Jesus' humanity and divinity can obviously bring clear direction to the liturgy. Such a **theme** can help to nail down choices for prayers, credal texts, readings, hymns, sermon, etc. Such a liturgy would be very clean, consistent and didactic.

- A **formational** concern might be to create the environment in which people can look at what God bids them do as brothers and sisters of Mary, Joseph and Jesus . . . and to turn in that direction. Such an **aim** opens up the possibility of testimony, dialogue, real-life drama and perhaps an act of dedication. Traditional liturgical elements such as the Magnificat or confession can spring to life. Such an approach is geared to changing lives rather than imparting knowledge. The Church might change too, perhaps not overnight but almost certainly with the experience of regular provision of such opportunities. The educational concern to impart an understanding of incarnation can still be met as a secondary goal.

Children and worship

Children are sensitive to the welcome the church offers to them as well as the welcome it offers their parents. The way in which adults are greeted, given service cards, chatted to and waved into church without a glance at the child at their side speaks volumes to children about how they are regarded at that church. Parents are also growing increasingly conscious of these subtle messages.

Welcoming children to church

- If you have a welcome desk for adults, set one up for
  children too at their height. Let some older children
  welcome the young people alongside the adult sidesmen
  and women. Provide interesting and creative colouring
  pictures and toys for children to take into church.
  Pictures that pick up a theme from the service can be
  very helpful to a child and can be presented to the
  congregation or at the altar as an offering from them.
  Don't insist that services are a play-free zone.
  Remember that young children will not stay engaged
  with a corporate activity all the time; make provision
  for them to disappear into some private play from time
  to time. Encourage the congregation to be tolerant of
  small children's noise and movement before, during and
  after the worship. Intangibles such as tolerance will
  impact on how far both youngsters and their adults feel
  welcomed.

Children are visually literate. They know when a service card is
designed with them in mind and they know when it isn't. Text
that looks as if it is lifted straight out of a newspaper belongs
to the world of adults, and children will readily switch off.
Child-friendly typefaces, colourful layout and pictures of or by
children are all devices that make a difference. Some children's
groups may actually be able to provide some of the decorative
artwork. In bookless services the OHP or PowerPoint® slides
can also be decorated with graphics by local children.

Church House Publishing and The National Society have
worked together to produce *The Communion Cube*.
This is a clever toy that changes in sequence into six
different forms. The shape of a communion service,
though not the words, can be followed through the
pictures and headings that are revealed as the cube is
manipulated. It is probably most suited to 3- to 6-year-old
children.

Children are able to give a lead to others in worship but, as with adults, whether they are prepared to do this or not will partly depend on the child's personality. Their role can vary from speaking some of the formal parts of the liturgy, such as prayers, to playing percussion or tuned instruments during songs and hymns, handing things out, acting as a server, etc.

There will also be times when, at least for part of the service, the children are together as a separate group to prepare their own contribution.

Children and adult collaboration

One simple way to encourage collaboration between a children's church and the adult church is to produce a collage representing everybody's unity in Christ. For instance:

- On Good Shepherd Sunday (Easter 4) have a stack of cut-out paper sheep prepared. As people arrive in church the children collect each of their signatures on a separate sheep. During the Liturgy of the Word the children can decorate these named sheep with cotton wool and stick them on a frieze to create a pastoral scene. This may also include a quote about Jesus as the Good Shepherd or a representation of him. Present the frieze later in the service as an image of the whole church community.

- On Good Friday provide sheets of black, brown and grey paper. Have children draw around one hand of each person who comes to church. Before the service finishes, some of the children can cut out the hands and stick them on a large sheet of paper in the shape of a cross. This can be presented in church as an icon of the sins of humanity that resulted in Christ's sacrifice.

- The Good Friday picture can be repeated on Easter Sunday with brightly coloured paper, glitter and sequins as an icon of the defeat of evil.

Many children learn their first songs in a simple register of music, which partly takes account of the tonal range of their voices and partly works through simple melodies and strong rhythms. These things need to be recognized in worship. Children will quickly pick up when music is not in their register and opt out of it. This is highly subjective and depends on age and experience, but worship planners need to be conscious of it.

Children are spiritual beings. They can respond to the numinous and can handle symbol. All-age worship shouldn't be designed to engage adults in confession, praise, intercession, etc., whilst the sermon slot is used to occupy the youngsters. Much more than the 'talk' can be made accessible to children by the use of appropriate language, action and presentation.

An Action Confession

Using actions along with the words of the liturgy can do much more than simply add a bit of fun to proceedings. Adults can use the actions to help convey something of the meaning of the words to the children. Children can use the actions to show their association with what is being said. The following confession is an example of how this can be done with words drawn out of Common Worship.

Before the prayer
everybody is asked to point behind themselves at ←,
point to themselves at ↓ and ahead at →:

Most merciful God,
Father of our Lord Jesus Christ,
we confess that we have sinned
in thought, word and deed.
We have not loved you with our whole heart.
We have not loved our neighbours as ourselves.
In your mercy
← forgive what we have been,
↓ help us to amend what we are,
→ and direct what we shall be;
that we may do justly,
love mercy,
and walk humbly with you, our God.
Amen.
(Words from New Patterns for Worship *B37, page 83)*

Working with an age range

There can be a tendency to underestimate the capacity of children to engage with issues of life and faith and also often a tendency to overestimate what adults can manage. A bright eleven-year-old can be ahead of the average adult in some congregations in their knowledge. In reality there are not many adults who can concentrate through a twenty-minute sermon, although most will pretend that they can. Children behave quite differently and will not feign interest quite so readily.

There are a host of strategies that can be adopted to try to keep the whole congregation at an all-age service all travelling along together in roughly the same direction. Some of these are listed below, but not all of them are equally useful or beneficial. This is not really a guide to what should be done but offers some ideas that can be used from time to time. Be careful though. *New Patterns for Worship* rightly mocks the overuse and lazy use of some of these strategies by St Dodo's! A snatch from the life of this hapless church is printed below as a warning.

Children at St Dodo's

Today is the monthly 'All-Age service' at **St Dodo's**, to which children and families have been invited, and there is a baptism. The young people are taking part in a drama (the Good Samaritan – again!) but once this is over they get restless, as the rest of the service is not especially geared to them. The baptism sounds like a long monologue, and the music consists of Victorian hymns that are all unfamiliar. The children in the Sunday School have been asked to lead the prayers, so the Sunday School teachers have written them on pieces of paper, and the children have some difficulty reading them. It is also difficult to hear what they are saying as the microphone is not adjusted to their height. There are some Bible story books (given to the church ten years ago) and colouring things at the back of church, but most of the children are now too old for them, and feel that they have rather outgrown such entertainment.

New Patterns for Worship, page 41.

If any of the strategies which follow were always relied upon, things might get too stratified. If people begin to sense that this element is for me and these other elements are for other people, the sense of being a single church can be lost. On the other hand, when your resources are being stretched, you need simple strategies just to keep people's interest alive.

Keeping interest alive

❑ Provide a great deal of age-specific activity throughout the worship (geared at little children or big children or teenagers or young adults or the more mature) but only in short bursts. This means that those who don't feel it particularly relates to them don't have time to get bored or finish counting the beams in the roof.

❑ Give the children a bag of toys or a picture to colour in. This means that when the adults are being addressed they can turn around, kneel down, lean on the pew or seat and do their own thing. This can still allow collaboration between adults and children, especially where themed toys and books are offered rather than simply what comes to hand. You can easily find pictures to colour in that can be shown as an integral part of the service and enable youngsters to lead the adults for a while. (Be aware that toys are age-specific and avoid noisy toys that can put parents on edge.)

❑ Aim everything at the middle-of-the-range children. The adults may remain interested enough and the younger children catch hold of at least a sense of fun about things.

❑ Use an overhead projector or a computer display projector to facilitate games and quizzes. Crosswords, word searches and pictograms can all encourage a wide range of participation. Be careful when presenting the words of the liturgy and the words of songs on the same screen, because children can find more distractions that way than they might with a song book or service card. On the other hand, projecting pictures in parallel with the words of intercession may help focus prayer better than 'hands together and eyes closed'. And children may enjoy managing the slides on an OHP for you, whilst also gaining respect among adults for doing so. Older teenagers may be better at managing a computer display projector than most adults.

❏ Puppets can be used in a number of ways. You can just tell stories to the eight-year-olds while holding a puppet to amuse the four-year-olds, and with the occasional joke that only the adults will understand. Used well, puppets can say and do things that adults or children could not otherwise get away with.

❏ Split into age-related groups during the service. Children may not need to be the ones that leave the church. Sometimes the adults could go and meet in a different room, and then the groups can come together again and even share with each other what they have been doing.

By adopting these sorts of strategies it is possible to keep a diverse group of people together in some sort of common experience of worship. This has value and is to some extent quite counter-cultural, because it demonstrates that the Church sees value in the insights and experiences of every human age, not just the physically and economically strong. In this it is being true to a saviour who held up children as icons of the Kingdom of God and lived as a suffering servant.

But the liturgy can do so much more than simply make an occasion together tolerable. *New Patterns for Worship* sets a much higher target than simply keeping people interested. Making worship come alive is the real goal.

Moving out of an educational mindset into worship mode is one key to this. The cautious strategies above relate mainly to moments when people are learning together, rather than to times when they are worshipping together. Where worship life is the focus, a whole new set of possibilities comes into play:

Making worship live

• Children like ritual. They will respond well to rhythm and repetition. Use taught responses in preference to written ones and let them flow throughout a service. So for instance you can punctuate a Mothering Sunday service from beginning to end with:

Praise God who loves us.
Praise God who cares.

(Words from *New Patterns For Worship* Sample Services)

Or you can use the CW Easter greeting in the same way:

Alleluia. Christ is risen!
He is risen indeed! Alleluia.

The pantomime aspect of this may help keep everyone on their toes – never sure when the phrase is going to come up again. Attention is galvanized by the congregation's desire not to be caught out and the sentence can become so well committed to peoples' memories that it will stay with them for a long time later.

- Use music that has repeated choruses or lines – it doesn't have to have been written as children's music. Some hymns do this, e.g. 'Guide me O thou great redeemer'. It was a device that the Wesleys used strongly in writing music that appealed to a wide cross-section. Today's songs for adults and children that can be used as rounds work in the same way. If there are people in your church who have the ability, try them singing verses as a cantor over a regularly repeated Taizé chorus such as Ubi Caritas.[1] There are settings for the Psalms where a sung chorus can be repeated after every two or three verses of spoken psalm. The music can be played quietly over the spoken words as a way of maintaining continuity and rhythm. Those written by Carey Landrey[2] work particularly well with children.

- Familiarity helps. Just like adults, children like to know where they are up to and where they are going, but may not be prepared to follow a service card in the same way. Keep a balance between the regular and the new. Elements of the liturgy that are used regularly enough to be committed to memory will help.

- Adults can help children to learn parts of the liturgy such as the Lord's Prayer but will need help in seeing this as their role.

This may mean something as simple as their saying to children, 'Do this with me', rather than, 'Don't do that!' Many adults will need to be taught to respond to children in this way.

- Being child friendly doesn't mean that adults must cringe. Be adult friendly too.

- Don't make children's leaders into policemen. Help all adults in a church to understand children and help to keep them on task. Help them also to develop their tolerance and, if distracted, to regard this as their problem rather than the children's fault. This doesn't mean telling the adults off, but encouraging them along.

- If the children spend some of their time in groups and some time worshipping with their parents, encourage the leaders not to abandon them in church. Leaders can help the parents (but be conscious that Junior Church leaders may expect to use the time they have in adult church for their own worship without the burden of worrying about the children).

- On the whole it helps to have adults alongside children during worship, but remember that children like to be seated with their peers. If possible, don't use adults to split them up but just to be within reach.

- Older children and young adults can connect easily with some symbolism and action, e.g. candles, chants, incense, and can communicate through them to other adults. For instance, teenagers can offer round baskets of pebbles at the beginning of a communion and encourage the adults to build a cairn centred on a candle as they return from receiving. This builds connections between the natural environment, the congregation as living stones and the idea of a church being built around Christ.

- Children like action and noise, but the adults don't have to join in. If youngsters dance in the aisles during a song, the adults may enjoy the children's worship if they're not forced to do the same.

- Appeal to more than one sense at a time if you can. Colour, sound and smell are often under-used. Simple things such as having music played under spoken words or pictures projected on a screen during prayers can help all ages. There are traditional symbols that can help too; for instance, incense burning in an open bowl in the middle of the church can be a reminder of prayers ascending.

For all ages

Although we have concentrated in this chapter on the role of children in all-age worship, because that is often the distinctive mark of this type of worship and the area where most of the obvious difficulties occur, it is also important to remember what was said at the beginning: the people who come to church may be 'of all ages, including the very aged and the very young'. The elderly also have their special needs and sometimes require help and understanding to enable them to take their full part in all-age worship. Service cards in large print, hearing loops for the deaf, and access for wheelchairs are three obvious things that can be done. But helping the elderly to make a contribution to the service – perhaps by asking them to pray for the speaker during his or her talk, or to share their testimony – is also important.

Older members of the congregation can often also strike up very positive relationships with children, more so than people of their parents' age. With a little bit of thought, it should be possible to set up some good interaction between the generations, both within the liturgy and outside it. If you are giving sweets or other prizes to children during the service, consider asking a senior member of the congregation to give them out. In the order for the Seder Eucharist described at the end of the next chapter, a senior member of the gathering can act as honorary parent and preside over some of the gathering, hiding matza parcels for children to find and giving out Easter eggs to those who find them.

So all-age services should be primarily about helping young and old to worship together. Through the worship they can open up the truths of God's kingdom to each other and be drawn into a closer relationship with God who renews and changes the kingdom's people.

3 Eucharistic all-age worship

Since 1997 children's experience of Holy Communion has begun to change radically across the Church of England. In January of that year the final form of the House of Bishops' guidelines on the admission of children to communion was published. The Anglican Churches of Canada, New Zealand, Australia and South Africa were ahead of the Church of England, and in the 1980s the dioceses of Manchester, Peterborough and Southwark had already negotiated some semi-official experimental patterns to facilitate this.

The Church's change of mind

The following is an extract from *Children and Holy Communion*.[1] This book offers good advice to churches considering the admission of children to communion and a six-week course for a children's group.

> The convincing arguments in favour of a change in practice seem to have been
>
> - the nature of baptism
>
> - the acceptance of children in the church
>
> - children's needs for spiritual nourishment
>
> - children's need to belong
>
> - the need of adults to 'become a child'.
>
> The bishops address the nature of baptism in these terms: 'The entire profession of the Christian life . . . is represented

in the action of baptism' (House of Bishops GS1212). In other words, baptism makes us full members of the Body of Christ.

It is on the basis of the baptism that we are bidden to express our membership in the receiving of the bread and the wine at Holy Communion. To exclude the children is therefore to deny their baptism.

Jesus' acceptance of children was explicit and particular:

They brought children to him to touch. The disciples rebuked them, but when Jesus saw this he was indignant, and said to them, 'Let the children come to me, and do not try to stop them; for the kingdom of God belongs to such as these.' And he put his arms round them, laid his hands upon them, and blessed them. (Mark 10: 13, 14, 16)

The Church is being challenged to be as welcoming and accepting of children as Jesus was.

Children's need for spiritual nurture is often interpreted as a requirement to teach a body of knowledge or an explicit moral code; far more is required, however. Children grow up as members of communities, assimilating the values and habits of the adults around them as well as of their peer group. We can teach them whatever we like about being a Christian, but their experience of the Christian people around them will far outweigh what they have been told. Similarly their experience of the Christian life – the joy of fellowship with other Christians, the excitement of the great festivals, the support in time of need and the regular pattern of encounter with God in prayer and sacrament – will all become part of the fabric of their lives in a way that what they are told about will not.

We all need to belong, and seldom stay in a place or group if we feel we don't belong there. This is especially true for children, who increasingly have the experience of leaving groups that don't meet their needs. Children in the seven-to-eleven-year-old age group have a great enjoyment of being part of a group, in particular one which contains adults too. It is an age when they will feel keenly any action which denies their membership or fails to include them. At this time they need to be active participants in those activities which define the group; any exclusion must be very clearly thought out and well understood if the church community is not to reap in teenage years the lack of involvement and poor quality of relationship sown in these crucial early years.

'I tell you, whoever does not accept the kingdom of God like a child will never enter it' (Mark 10: 15). Jesus challenges us not only to welcome children wholeheartedly into the church, but to cherish the way they belong to the kingdom and to be like them. It is the experience of many who have knelt at the altar in the presence of children that these words strike home keenly and take on a powerful resonance.

The presence of children in worship, who are as much a part of the communicant body as anybody else, poses a number of challenges to a liturgy that has often revolved around the needs of adults. Quite a lot of the principles outlined in the previous pages for non-eucharistic worship can be applied to some parts of the service. This might especially be the case for the Liturgy of the Word where three readings and a Psalm are rarely going to be appropriate. But what about the Liturgy of the Sacrament? An adult congregation may need to adjust some of its expectations.

- It is a common practice for young people to meet separately from adults for the 'first half' of a communion service. ASOTW with Holy Communion makes it possible to organize the liturgy in a way that helps adults and children to be together for the whole service from time to time. Neither children nor adults who have become used to a pattern of meeting separately will necessarily look forward to this with enthusiasm. You may need to work especially hard at appropriate preparation for such a service. It will undoubtedly be done best in collaboration with the children's leaders and even the children themselves.

- Where members of a junior church meet separately for the Liturgy of the Word but join the adults for communion, their leaders can make use of the ASOTW provision to shape their gathering, even if the adults use one of the standard rites. It is perfectly acceptable for a lay person to do this, providing that an episcopally ordained priest presides over the Liturgy of the

Sacrament and the Dismissal. People taking on the role of leading 'ante-communion' in children's groups might not have the gifts to do so instinctively. Churches hoping to develop this may well have to think through their training needs.

- When adults and children meet separately for some of the time, consider leaving the children in church on occasion and having the adults depart to groups.

- When adults and children have been meeting separately and join together for communion, give some attention to the moment of meeting. Children will not feel valued if they simply enter during a hymn and are ignored. You could occasionally invite them to show what they have been doing in their group to the adults and ask someone to explain to the youngsters what the adults have been thinking about.

- The response of adults to children at the Peace is as important as the welcome into church that they receive (see pages 26–7). Encourage the adults to smile at children and under no circumstances to overlook or ignore them. Children themselves are very aware of relationships with their own peers. They could be encouraged to use the Peace as a time to 'make up' with friends with whom they have fallen out. But be aware that some children may be as reticent as some adults to join in with the Peace.

- The Preparation of the Table is a good moment for children to lead and serve the adults. The words of offertory from CW Order One (below) are particularly appropriate when children bring forward the bread and wine:

With this bread that we bring
we shall remember Jesus.

With this wine that we bring
we shall remember Jesus.

Bread for his body,
wine for his blood
gifts from God to his table we bring.
We shall remember Jesus.

Common Worship *Supplementary Texts: Prayers at Preparation of Table*

These words need printing out for the congregation or projecting on a screen. They work well if a child who has carried bread forward leads the first response, a child who has carried wine forward leads the second, and the president leads the third. The children will probably speak with their backs to the congregation so a microphone can help if there is one to hand. They may need the words printing in large letters on a card. Place this on a music stand nearby as they will each need two hands to carry the bread and wine.

Preambles before the Eucharistic Prayer

A child might ask the questions, which the president or deacon might answer, and not all questions need be attempted every time.

Q Why do we give thanks and praise to God?

A Because he has created all that is, and he has given us life. He is Lord of all, and yet loves each of us.

Q Why do we remember Jesus?

A Because he was sent from God and he gave up his life for us on the cross. God raised him from the dead so that we might see that death is not the end, but the beginning of a new life, the life Jesus showed us how to live.

Q Why do we use bread?

A Because Jesus took bread at the Last Supper. It is a sign of Jesus feeding us as we share with others around his table.

Q Why do we use wine?

A Because this wine is a sign of Jesus' saving love, poured out for us when he died on the cross.

New Patterns for Worship, page 42

Another way that *New Patterns for Worship* suggests children can contribute to the adults' appreciation of the Eucharist is borrowed from the Jewish tradition. At a Passover meal it is usual for a child to ask the oldest member of the family some questions about the reasons for the celebration. *New Patterns* suggests some forms of preamble that may be asked about communion. (See the panel on the opposite page for an example.)

Whatever happens, the actions, style and approach of the president, while being accessible to children, should make clear that the whole prayer is addressed to God, in whose presence it is right to be filled with awe. The sense of mystery should not lose out to a chatty educational or instructional approach.

- Two of the Order One eucharistic prayers were written with children in mind. Neither conforms to what will have been familiar to adults prior to Common Worship. Prayer D is written in a language and poetic rhythm that is particularly close to the responsive words of offertory printed above. It may also lend itself well to some new and novel musical settings for the repeated responses. Prayer H is short and highly responsive. Adults sometimes find this prayer particularly strange because of its structure and because it finishes with the Sanctus. People who expect this in the middle of the prayer sometimes think it can't have finished when it has. The responses are all different from each other and may be tricky for young children. The content of Prayer H is very comfortable, saying little of pain, suffering and the cross. Inevitably, texts such as these, written for contexts involving children, have not been part of the Church's tradition before and will jar with some people. But it is worth looking out for times when they are particularly appropriate to meet the needs of the moment.

- All-age Communion services are bound to include both adults and children who are not ready to receive communion. Many will come to the altar rail for a blessing. Hidden away in *New Patterns for Worship* are some new suggestions for words that may be used here. See the box on the following page.

Blessings

Where children and adults who are not receiving communion are being blessed at the rail, it is good to vary the form of words used. Some possibilities are:

- The Lord bless you and keep you;

- The Lord bless you and give you joy in all you do for him;

- The Lord bless and take care of you *both* (for example, with a married couple when one of them is receiving communion and the other not);

- The Lord bless and strengthen you as you seek to follow him (especially suitable for those preparing for baptism or confirmation);

- Christ fill you with his joy and peace;

- The blessing of Jesus Christ rest upon you;

- May God be with you;

- May Jesus Christ bless you.

New Patterns for Worship, Resource Section I, pages 283–4

- In some churches it will take a long time for everybody to receive Holy Communion. If the adults have gravitated to the seats at the back, the children will almost certainly be sitting at the front and will come to the altar rail first. They will then have a long time to wait and fidget whilst others want some space to reflect. This needs thinking through. The right choice of music can make a very big difference. Toys for young children and word searches for those of junior age can help a great deal.

Exeter Diocese produces a '*Young Church Mag*' aimed at children in the choir or congregation. It is based on the CW lectionary, with colouring sheets, crosswords, quizzes, etc. This is available nationally on an annual subscription for local photocopying. It can occupy lively minds in ways consistent with worship.

- *New Patterns for Worship* provides some prayers that it calls 'triple solemn blessings'. Children can respond very well to these providing they are used in a way that is anything but solemn. The repeated use of 'amen' in the prayer lends itself well to a crescendo. The name suggests that they contain three 'amens', but in reality they have four and are best used immediately before words of dismissal that also end in 'amen'. So typically a service can end with something like the following (see *New Patterns for Worship* Resource Section J, p. 303):

The Lord bless you and keep you.
Amen.

The Lord make his face to shine upon you,
and be gracious to you.
Amen.

The Lord look on you with favour
and give you peace.
Amen.

The Lord God almighty, Father, Son, and Holy Spirit,
the holy and undivided Trinity,
guard you, save you,
and bring you to that heavenly city,
where he lives and reigns for ever and ever.
AMEN.

Go in peace to love and serve the Lord.

In the name of Christ. AMEN.

Used with groups of adults without any preparation, this sort of prayer can end in a whimper as the 'amens' get progressively quieter and more uncertain. Children, asked to make each 'amen' louder than the last, can give such prayers a real lift. You could print the last two responses in capitals as a visual cue to this but it also helps to brief the children verbally.

Free but still moored

A Service of the Word makes it possible for services of Holy Communion to be tailored to local needs as easily as non-eucharistic worship. This can be anything from a gentle reorganization or substitution of one or two texts to a wholesale re-ordering of everything before the Peace. *New Patterns* provides a great deal of additional material that can be used.

The two orders of Holy Communion printed in *Common Worship*, each in contemporary and traditional language, have a great deal of flexibility of content. In these services the Sermon can take on a variety of forms and the Prayers of Intercession are almost limitlessly flexible. There are no less than thirteen Eucharistic Prayers / Prayers of Consecration, some of them with as many as sixteen seasonal variations. Such is the freedom offered by these 'normative' rites that the additional provision of A Service of the Word with a Celebration of Holy Communion is preceded by the rubric,

> *This rite requires careful preparation by the president and other participants, and is not normally to be used as a regular Sunday or weekday service.*

For the sake of a coherent Church there undoubtedly needs to be some consistency in the worship texts that shape its members' understandings of communion. But there is still a strong argument for the existence of ASOTW with a Celebration of Holy Communion service, particularly in the case of all-age worship, which is the subject of this chapter, provided that the desire of the wider Church for consistency is understood.

This service structure offers considerable freedom. It is printed in full in the table alongside and you will see that there are only three sections that must follow an authorized form (an asterisk* in the table denotes those texts that must be authorized):

- the Prayers of Penitence;
- the Collect;
- and the Eucharistic Prayer.

Service Structure

*A Service of the Word
with a Celebration of Holy Communion*

Preparation

The people and the priest:

¶   greet each other in the Lord's name
¶   confess their sins and are assured of God's forgiveness*
¶   keep silence and pray a Collect*

The Liturgy of the Word

The people and the priest:

¶   proclaim and respond to the word of God

Prayers

The people and the priest:

¶   pray for the Church and the world

The Liturgy of the Sacrament

The people and the priest:

¶   exchange the Peace
¶   prepare the table
¶   pray the Eucharistic Prayer*
¶   break the bread
¶   receive Holy Communion

The Dismissal

The people and the priest:

¶   depart with God's blessing

Agape or Seder

The practice of sharing in Holy Communion during the course of
a meal was first introduced into the semi-official liturgy of the
Church of England in *Lent, Holy Week and Easter*, published in
1985. This brought the Eucharist into a living setting that had

some equivalence with the way the earliest Christians would have experienced it. It is now also quite common for churches to share the Eucharist over a meal that also incorporates many of the symbols of a traditional Jewish Passover meal. This can be of strong significance on Maundy Thursday in particular. When communion is celebrated in the course of a normal English meal, it seems to be known as an *Agape* and when elements of modern Judaism are also imported into it, the Jewish name of *Seder* is also often borrowed.

Real all-age worship can quite easily be achieved on such occasions. Young and old alike can respond to the informality of the meal and the interpretations of the Eucharist. When some elements of contemporary Judaism are added, many of them unfamiliar to British Christians, children can be even more drawn into events. If you want to develop an event along these lines, it helps to have a book to 'hold your hand' along the way. There are quite a number of guides available which give good Christian interpretations of the Seder. See Appendix 1 for details.

A Service of the Word with a Celebration of Holy Communion can easily be used as the basis for a Seder celebration in church. The panel at the end of this chapter makes some suggestions about order. The catering needs serious thought and it can be difficult to encourage the kitchen helpers to feel thoroughly involved in the worship event. Children may well be prepared to help them out, perhaps by serving at the table. You can sit people in groups around small tables, but, if you have the space to make a large oblong out of trestle tables and sit everybody around it in one group, the sense of fellowship can be stronger. A coffee table on the floor in the centre of such an oblong can carry two or three candles (to be lit at the beginning) and a display, perhaps of a cross and an open Bible as a focus for the people.

In conclusion, ASOTW offers a number of ways in which children can engage more comfortably with a Communion service. It can be used as ante-communion in separate groups before they gather with the rest of the church for the Liturgy of the Sacrament. It can also be used to construct liturgies which help children and adults to worship together and lead each other.

An outline Seder following ASOTW with a Celebration of Holy Communion

This outline is only a sketch and will not be adequate to follow if you are organizing an event, but it should help you to be selective from the myriad of possibilities that the more specific books on the subject will offer. It can be quite difficult to keep some coherence and parallels with the more usual experiences of communion that people are likely to have. Without this, the event can lose its point of making the Eucharist come alive. The occasion can benefit from a well-read and well-briefed narrator who keeps some interpretation running throughout. It is probably best if this person is not the President. It can work well if the narrator is also responsible for all the readings from Scripture.

The ¶ symbol denotes a section required by ASOTW and words in italics are lifted from Jewish practice. Songs and hymns can be sung throughout. In the use of music, it may be helpful to retain some parallel with the more usual pattern for your church, as this can help people keep tabs on where you have got to (e.g. Opening hymn, gradual, offertory and concluding hymn). No particular recommendations are made about music below.

Four cups of wine are traditionally drunk during a Seder and you may want to make some alternative provision for the children. These cups are:

- to life

- to freedom

- of redemption, and

- to the future.

The order below parallels the third cup with the cup of Christian Eucharist. Other interpretations are possible.

Order of Service

¶ Preparation   *Festival of Candle Lighting:*

A woman may typically light two candles with some words of blessing. In the church setting you may light three candles with a Trinitarian formula such as *New Patterns A20*.

Kiddush: The cup to life.

Urehatz: A reminder of purity. This may involve a remembrance in word and action of Jesus' foot-washing and some words of confession (e.g. *New Patterns B48*) and absolution (e.g. *New Patterns B78*)

The Peace

Collect

¶ The Liturgy of the Word

¶ Intersperse the following elements with readings from Exodus, the epistles (e.g. 1 Corinthians 5:7) and the Passion Narratives.

Karpas: A reminder of the bitterness of slavery involving the eating of bitter green herbs.

Yachatz: A reminder of brokenness involving the hiding of broken Matzot bread for children to find later.

Maggid: The cup of memory. This may also include:

* questions asked by youngsters and answered by the assembly about the meaning of Passover,

* interpretation of some Passover symbols (a lamb's shank-bone, matzot and bitter herbs),

* the Hillel sandwich, which is itself a reminder of slave labour: matzot and almond paste as representation of bricks and mortar.

Prayers

¶ Pray for the Church and the world

¶ The Liturgy of the Sacrament

The Meal

Tzafun: the children search for hidden bread and receive prizes.

¶ Clear and prepare the table

The Third Cup to Redemption

¶ Pray the Eucharistic Prayer

¶ Break bread

¶ Receive Holy Communion

¶ The Dismissal

Neertza: the fourth cup to the future

Final Benediction
End by saying together:
Next year in Jerusalem!

4 Morning and Evening Prayer

The use of Morning and Evening Prayer in the Church of England goes back to the Church's birth in the Reformation period and has a history that extends to the earliest days of Christian worship. The services consist of psalms, readings, canticles and prayers, with provision for a sermon and a liturgical introduction and conclusion. Morning and Evening Prayer on Sunday may not be used so much today in parishes where there is a strong eucharistic tradition, but they are still familiar and well-loved services, especially in many rural churches which may not have a eucharistic celebration every week.

Common Worship contains the services of Morning Prayer on Sunday and Evening Prayer on Sunday in both contemporary language and BCP versions. The contemporary language versions also draw on many recent developments in liturgical thinking. They are printed only as sample services to demonstrate one way that ASOTW can be used. They are not definitive and prescriptive but are similar to the sample services in the third section of *New Patterns for Worship*. The fact that these sample forms of Morning and Evening Prayer are printed in *Common Worship* will undoubtedly mean that they will be used fairly heavily without any significant alteration. Some churches have bought this worship book in large enough numbers for everybody in church to be given a copy.

New Patterns also contains three further samples of general services which some churches may prefer to those in *Common Worship*; however, these will probably need to be printed out separately. They are:

• Morning Praise,

• For all the Church Family, and

• An Evening Service of the Word.

The three *New Patterns* sample services are much simpler than those offered in *Common Worship*. Canticle material is only included in the Morning Praise service (Venite) and no psalms are suggested other than those which might be included as readings from the Bible. Nevertheless, these bare bones undoubtedly provide a good framework to be fleshed out according to local needs.

All these published versions of Morning and Evening Prayer are not the last word but rather the first. They offer a good place to start, demonstrating how morning or evening prayer can be drawn from the resources that the Church of England provides via ASOTW. Of course, if you are not wedded to handing out copies of the official books to every member of the congregation you are free to think it out again. Before doing so, it is worth taking a moment to understand the rationale that has informed the samples on offer. The *New Patterns* samples have a number of clear and straightforward starting points:

• **Morning Praise (Sample Service 1)** encourages a start to the day in the conscious presence of God. So it uses words of praise that begin, 'O Lord, open my lips', and the use of the Venite, which bids its readers to 'come and sing' to the creator of the universe.

• **For all the Church Family (2)** draws worshippers into union with God as Trinity and with each other. Its focus is on how we relate together. Its language is simple and not wordy, making its use with very young children quite possible. So it includes a relationally focussed opening greeting which begins, 'Let us worship God, Father, Son and Holy Spirit', and prayers of confession which reflect the idea of 'behaviour' with a simple repeated response, 'Father, forgive us, **save us and help us.**'

• **An Evening Service of the Word (3)** connects with the evening as a time of darkness in which light becomes all the more important. So it begins with, 'The light and peace of Jesus Christ be with you'. The introduction to confession says,

'Christ the light of the world has come to dispel the darkness of our hearts. In his light let us examine ourselves and confess our sins,' and there is a 'Praise Response' that encourages reflection on the creator of the universe who has made night and day and who set the stars in their courses.

These very direct connections made with some of the simplest features of day-to-day life help to open up the imagination to much more. In themselves the services are uncomplicated and they invite the weaving in of additional strands. When you are preparing for worship based on these samples you will need to bring additional elements of fun or learning or spiritual resonance into the framework they offer.

The two contemporary sample services of Morning and Evening Prayer in *Common Worship* are of a more traditionally poetic type. They share something of the structure of the services in *Common Worship: Daily Prayer (Preliminary Edition)* and have deep roots in *Celebrating Common Prayer*, the ASB and BCP.

• **Morning Prayer on Sunday** resonates with the beginning of the day and the dawning of faith as it unfolds in anticipation of Christ through the Old Testament. This echoes through the liturgy from prayers such as the thanksgiving on page 32:

Blessed are you, Lord our God,
creator and redeemer of all;
to you be glory and praise for ever.
From the waters of chaos you drew forth the world
and in your great love fashioned us in your image.
Now, through the deep waters of death,
you have brought your people to new birth
by raising your Son to life in triumph.
May Christ your light ever dawn in our hearts
as we offer you our sacrifice of thanks and praise.
Blessed be God, Father, Son and Holy Spirit:
Blessed be God for ever.

The theme is continued in the seasonal selection of Old Testament canticles and reaches its high point in the Gospel Canticle, the Benedictus: 'This was the oath God swore to our father Abraham'.

- **Evening Prayer on Sunday**: the evening resonances are drawn from the New Testament, realizing Christ as the light that the darkness could not overcome. So the prayer of thanksgiving acclaims Christ, 'rising victorious, as he banishes all darkness from our hearts and minds' (p. 40). The high point of this liturgy is again the Gospel Canticle, this time the Magnificat, which praises God who has fulfilled 'the promise made to our ancestors, to Abraham and his children for ever'.

The connections made in these two services with the work of God in the lives of his people are many and complex. In communities where Morning and Evening Prayer throughout the week are a clear part of the pattern of life, they will fit well. Where they stand alone and are only used on occasional Sundays, they may seem dense and difficult to understand. If the rich traditions that help them make sense aren't present in the group of people who have gathered for worship, then their direction might just be confusing. In some places the right solution will be to teach the congregation where to find the resonances and how to pray in these ways. In other places it may be better to use simpler forms of prayer.

Forms of Thanksgiving

Common Worship provides four forms of Thanksgivings for Use at Morning and Evening Prayer on Sunday (pp. 46–56). (These can also be found in *Common Worship: Daily Prayer (Preliminary Edition)*, pp. 270–82.) They can be used to give some liturgical shape and action to the service after The Word of God, other than the recitation of a creed and intercessions. These thanksgivings have particular flavours and are not intended for constant regular use; but there will be occasions throughout the year when they might enrich people's opportunity to respond to God through worship. They each have slightly different structures and need to be used in different ways. They could easily be used at other times than at the end of a Sunday service of Morning or Evening Prayer, but when they are used with the *Common Worship* version of Morning or Evening Prayer, this is how it might work:

- **Thanksgiving for the Word** provides an opportunity for the congregation to make a variety of responses after their reading and reflection on the Word of God. One of the issues that has surrounded the Common Worship approach is that confession is normally regarded as belonging in the Preparation. This makes confession as a response to 'God's Word' less possible as part of the Church's developing pattern of worship. The *New Patterns* form of Thanksgiving offers a range of responses to the Word which include confession, testimony, intercession, sharing of the peace and proclamation.

  Thanksgiving for the Word should replace everything in Morning or Evening Prayer after the sermon. The confession should also be omitted from the Preparation.

- **Thanksgiving for Holy Baptism** enables the congregation to remember their baptism with thanks in word and action. People may simply be given the opportunity to make this response with little preparation other than the stimulus of readings and sermon on the day.

  However, it could also be the basis for a well-signalled annual opportunity such as the tradition that many churches maintain at Epiphany, Easter or Pentecost. This will work best if the whole congregation is invited to gather around the font after the sermon. From that point on the Thanksgiving replaces everything else in Morning or Evening Prayer. If you decide to sprinkle the congregation with water, it will help to have a formula of words to hand such as those offered in *The Promise of His Glory* (CHP, 1991), p. 222:

    Remember your baptism into Christ.
    Thanks be to God.

- **Thanksgiving for the Healing Ministry of the Church** provides an additional liturgical setting for the exercise of the healing ministry over and above those provided in *Common Worship: Pastoral Services*. In this case healing becomes quite a dominant focus of the service and it would probably help those attending if they are prepared for it before the day. The notes to the service clearly state that such ministry must only be undertaken by those authorized for it. This form of Thanksgiving can also be used without anointing or the laying on of hands, which may make it easier to be more spontaneous.

This Thanksgiving includes a possible reading from the Bible, and the sermon may be better placed after this rather than earlier in the service. This is simply a matter of replacing everything from Morning or Evening Prayer after the Gospel Canticle with this material.

- **Thanksgiving for the Mission of the Church** is an opportunity for people to reaffirm their commitment to the fellowship and mission of the Church. It might work well at a landmark or turning point in the local church's life or simply in response to issues raised through reading the Bible. It could be the focus of some healing after a moment of crisis. You can also choose to use this when people are taking on particular new ministries within the church, as it gives an opportunity for their commissioning.

There is definite provision for the reading of a Gospel at the beginning of this Thanksgiving. It may be that the sermon should also come after this, although that is not explicitly suggested in the text. Simply replace everything in Morning or Evening Prayer after the Gospel Canticle with this material.

The presence of these Thanksgivings in *Common Worship* makes them very accessible. When the congregation is using the book to follow the service, it is quite easy for them to turn on a few pages for one of these as an alternative ending. But they are also only examples of what can be done. They may well stretch your imagination to other possibilities and the freedoms of ASOTW give you the scope to try out those ideas too.

Modern or traditional?

The winds of change have been blowing through the Church of England and the currents of thinking about worship have changed considerably since the days of Series 3 or even the introduction of the ASB. Just 25 years later it is difficult to remember the outrage there was in some corners of England over the use of contemporary language in the established church. It was called 'modern language' then, but even that term seems a little bit old-fashioned now.

It may have been partly the sharpness of the debate that polarized liturgical practice. Services were thought of as being either modern language or traditional. A mix and match approach was frowned upon. Those who were driving the change to contemporary language knew that they had to effect a huge culture shift in the Church and a change in the nation's thinking about religion. No halfway house was going to be acceptable. A new Lord's Prayer was never going to catch on unless it was the only Lord's Prayer people used, and unless the language of prayer was once again in the same register as the language of conversation, the mission of the Church was always going to be impaired. On the other hand, some people recognized that the spiritual tradition of the Church of England was encapsulated in its forms of worship, which had nurtured Christian people and shaped the nation's culture for over four hundred years. They wanted to protect this heritage.

There were, of course, more theological issues and questions of poetic taste and decency. But, on the whole, the choice for one form of words or the other was most likely to be driven by your notion of mission. And there were only two positions to adopt, with no middle ground. The first edition of the ASB took the modern language line wholeheartedly and didn't even have provision for the use of a traditional Lord's Prayer in Rite A Communion. This was introduced by a later decision of the General Synod.

Today the debate has softened, and as a consequence the irritation once felt by members of the Church when the 'wrong' words were used has died down. Words that were considered antiquated by one camp or brazen by the other can now be comfortably used with most people. Services no longer need to be flagged up as traditional or modern. While they may be advertised as Common Worship, this no longer carries any of the old associations of a particular form of language.

Nowadays, Morning and Evening Prayer may offer the most suitable context for some mixed language usage, and there would seem to be little cause now for condemning this. Amongst the regular offices of the Church these are the services that tend to most affected by resonances of the past and hope for what lies ahead. The same may also be true of a number of the occasional offices, such as weddings and funerals. It is probably on these sorts of occasions that the language of the Prayer Book is still valued, even in the most twenty-first century churches. Somehow it evokes a sense of transcendence and timeless continuity. Used alongside contemporary words, both direct and poetic, traditional formulae can help people into the presence of the God who is both transcendent and immanent. It can express the God who is of both all generations and the here and now.

This sort of movement can be seen in the return to words from the Marriage Service such as, 'Those whom God has joined together let no one put asunder'. Words from the past can sometimes express a hope or desire beyond our own immediate power better than an everyday word might.

When you are working with ASOTW it may help to be alert to this. You won't find any prayers in *New Patterns* which retain completely the language of the sixteenth century, but that shouldn't stop you from turning to other sources you know best. You will find lightly revised prayers in *New Patterns* that retain their Cranmerian resonances. For instance,

Almighty God, Father of all mercies,
we your unworthy servants
   give you most humble and hearty thanks
for all your goodness and loving kindness.
We bless you for our creation, preservation,
   and all the blessings of this life;
but above all for your immeasurable love
in the redemption of the world by our Lord Jesus Christ,
for the means of grace, and for the hope of glory.
And give us, we pray, such a sense of all your mercies
that our hearts may be unfeignedly thankful,
and that we may show forth your praise,
not only with our lips but in our lives,
by giving up ourselves to your service,
and by walking before you in holiness
   and righteousness all our days;
through Jesus Christ our Lord
to whom, with you and the Holy Spirit,
   be all honour and glory,
for ever and ever.
Amen.

New Patterns for Worship, Resources G57

Stepping out just a little

The character of Morning and Evening Prayer is that they provide a framework for prayer that is in tune with the rhythms of creation. Worship of this sort is like bracketing the day in prayer. There are, of course, more motifs than the dawning of God's truth and his enlightening of our spirits (cf. Morning and Evening Prayer) that resonate with our daily experiences of creation.

ASOTW gives real encouragement to look beyond the familiar scenery of the Church of England. It offers a mandate to step out a little. And to those churches well used to stepping out, ASOTW gives sanction to what they have been doing.

Stepping out doesn't necessarily mean heading off into virgin territory. There are a great number of paths that can be found and explored just a little way off the Common Worship motorway. Some of these are published and some you will discover more locally. Many of them spring out of the life of religious communities, which have long felt free to be more liturgically innovative than most parish churches. Worship is used to give shape to their day and much of this prayer is organized for use every day of the week and year. It is difficult simply to transfer such daily prayer into a weekly rhythm or for occasional use when there may be no rhythm at all. Some of it can be used as a resource for special occasions, like the material discussed below, which has been produced specifically for this purpose.

The territory is so enormous that we can do no more here than point out some of the most prominent features on the landscape.

Taizé

Taizé is an ecumenical community in the Burgundy region of France. Its numbers are often swollen by large numbers of visitors, young and old, who are seeking spiritual refreshment and encouragement. Worship is at the heart of the community's witness.

The worship of Taizé is often very musical and characterized by repetitive harmonized choruses and chants. Much of this material has been widely published. The community also produces a great number of prayer resources with liturgical ideas and advice. Brother Roger describes their approach to worship in these terms:

> Caught up in the anonymous rhythms of schedules and timetables, men and women of today are implicitly thirsting for the one essential reality: an inner life, signs of the invisible. Nothing is more conducive to a communion with the living God than a meditative common prayer with, as its high point, singing that never ends and that continues in the silence of one's heart when one is alone again. When the mystery of God becomes tangible through the simple beauty of symbols, when it is not smothered by too many words, then a common prayer, far from exuding monotony and boredom, awakens us to heaven's joy on earth.[1]

The book, *Songs and Prayers from Taizé* (Mowbray, 1991), offers a simple entry point into this Taizé approach. It is organized a little like *New Patterns*, with an outline structure for 'a time of prayer' followed by resources organized in sections that fit with the structure headings.

Outline structure for Taizé prayers

- One or two opening songs
- Psalm
- Song of light (optional)
- First Bible reading
- Song
- Second Bible reading
- Silence
- Prayer of intercession or adoration
- Lord's Prayer
- Concluding Prayer
- Meditative songs

- Prayer around the cross (optional)

- Celebration of the resurrection (optional)

This form of prayer fits with the structure of ASOTW, except that on Sunday and Principal Holy Days ASOTW expects to have a sermon. However, given the wide interpretation of 'sermon', appropriate use of prayer and meditative material interspersed with song could fulfil this need.

Iona

The Iona Community draws a range of people from many countries and denominations into an expression of common life lived out wherever they may be. This is demonstrated in a rule of daily prayer, Bible reading and use of time and money that revolves around concerns for justice and peace. The founders of the community worked in areas of poverty in Glasgow, and its genesis was in the rebuilding of the ancient monastic abbey buildings on the island of Iona. The community maintains three centres in the Western Isles and its main base is a community house in Glasgow.

The Iona Community gave birth to the Wild Goose Worship and Resource Group which has been prolific in the production of music and liturgical resources. One of their strengths is the way their worship resources hold together a sense of wonder in God's creation and the realities of urban living.

Among the earliest of their publications was *A Wee Worship Book* (Wild Goose Worship Resource Group, 2nd edn 2002), which contains a number of orders and forms for morning and evening prayer services. Whilst many of these are intended for regular use, they are easily adapted for particular occasions. *The Pattern of Our Days* (ed. Kathy Galloway, 1996) contains over eighty pages of liturgy and a further eighty pages of prayer resources which carry deep resonances with the varied experiences of day-to-day life.

Prayer from the Iona Community

The knees of our hearts we bow

In the sight of God who created us,
In the sight of the son who died for us,
In the sight of the Spirit who helps us,
In friendship and affection.

Through your own Son, O Maker of all,
grant us the fullness our lives long for:

Love for God,
Love from God,
The smile of God,
The grace of God,
The wisdom of God,
The fear of God,
The imagination of God,
And God's purpose in all things.

So may we live in this world
As saints and angels do in heaven.

Each shadow and light,
Each day and night,
Each moment in kindness,
Give us your Spirit.
Amen.

From 'Evening Liturgy C', *A Wee Worship Book*

World Church music and prayers

A sense of wonder in the created order seems to be diminishing in the Western world, especially in urban communities. In places where the streets are bright whether it be day or night, and where the supermarkets can sell fresh strawberries all year round, humanity might seem to have overcome the elements. This is not so in every corner of the world. Sometimes the assumptions that undergird the prayers, music and liturgies of one culture can help people in other cultures see themselves in a new relation to God and creation. The poetic rhythms of other languages can stimulate the senses. A foreign musical register can help people express themselves before God in ways that the Victorian hymn writers couldn't have conceived.

So the 'Peruvian Gloria' might replace a traditional canticle, or African music be used to bring a sense of joy and dance to worship. It may be that some words from a Kenyan liturgy are able to express the people's relation to the earth or that prayers from the Church of South India will help them reflect on their relation to those whose views are different from their own. And beyond the words and music of the world Church it is possible to use the whole liturgy of another culture. All of these can bring about a much deeper sense of both humanity's immense diversity and its shared experience. This enriches the local church's sense of the creator.

Most of the provinces of the Anglican Communion have written their own prayer books and these often fit easily within the provision of ASOTW. There is a great deal of world Church music available. See also *Let All the World* (USPG, 1990), a book of complete liturgies, litanies, prayers and music drawn from numerous sources around the world.

Prayers of Repentance from the Church of Kenya

Almighty God,
Creator of the living and the non-living,
you marvellously made us in your image;
but we have corrupted ourselves
and damaged your likeness,
by rejecting your love
and hurting our neighbour.
We are desperately sorry
and heartily repent of our sins.
Cleanse us and forgive us
by the sacrifice of your Son;
Remake us and lead us
by your Spirit, the Comforter.
We only dare to ask this
through Jesus Christ our Lord.
Amen.

Church of the Province of Kenya

The Mothers' Union

In 1995 the Mothers' Union published their *Worship Book* to augment the 1974 *Mothers' Union Service Book*. In this new book there is advice on planning a service, a number of new liturgies and a resources section. Their concerns are to make good connections between faith and daily life. This is done in a way that resonates well with the English spirit. Along with the inevitable services to enrol members and officers and services to celebrate aspects of married and family life, the *Worship Book* also includes services for the morning, midday and the afternoon or evening. It all fits within the framework of ASOTW and could be used in a range of contexts including small Sunday services.

A summer prayer

We thank you, Loving Father,
for the joys that summer brings:
for warm days and soft breezes,
for the trees and the flowers,
for the freedom to wear tee shirts and summer dresses,
for open doors and meals outside.
Help us to remember that all lovely things come from you.

The Mothers' Union Worship Book

Symbols for the morning and the evening

The catalogue of symbols used for Morning or Evening Prayer in many churches is often very short indeed. These services are often conducted in a dour and static way with little for the eye to rest upon except perhaps for a minister in cassock and surplice with a prayer book in hand. Some churches may light a candle in the evening but there are others that most definitely won't because candles are reserved for the celebration of the Eucharist. (See the ideas panel on the next page.)

Symbols for Matins and Evensong

There is a great deal that can be done to speak to the eyes as well as the ears. It doesn't have to be complicated.

- Place the lectern in the centre of the gathering. If it has been in the one place in the church for centuries this can have quite an impact. If it appeared to be too heavy ever to move, the impact will be all the greater. This serves to focus people on the Bible as the Word of God around which they have assembled.

- Most churches use flowers as ornament. In services that reflect something of the cycle of time, try using plant life in stronger ways. Don't be restricted to the conventionally attractive. At times of penitence try using a display of weeds. In the winter you can use dead wood. Don't just keep such displays behind the altar. In the spring give children a seed to take away and plant at home.

- As a reminder of the damage that humanity can cause place a stack of broken and rusted things in the centre of the church. See *The Pattern of Our Days* (The Iona Community, 1996) for more ideas like this.

- Use the lighting carefully. Don't switch the church lights on for a morning service until the opening greeting. Keep the lighting subdued in the evening. Create pools of light with candles or lamps, perhaps around a cross or Bible.

- Use incense, though not necessarily swinging in a thuribel as at the Eucharist. Incense can be burnt in a bowl during the prayers, with the smoke simply rising. Words such as *New Patterns* Resources Section A16 interpret the symbol:

  > O Lord, we call to you: come to us quickly.
  > **Hear us when we cry to you.**

  > Let our prayers rise up before you like incense.
  > **Let our lifted hands be like an evening sacrifice.**

Glory to the Father and to the Son
and to the Holy Spirit;
as it was in the beginning is now
and shall be for ever. Amen.

Morning and Evening Prayer offer moments when people can
reflect on the cycle of time in the presence of God who is eternal.
This experience has a universal aspect. ASOTW encourages you
to bring all your capacity for colour, poetry, movement and
imagination to these moments, not as distractions to prayer but
to resonate with the numinous.

5 Worship between Sundays

Annual services such as Christingle Services, and one-off events such as centenaries, draw people into worship from beyond the circle of those who may attend week by week. There are also times in the 'secular calendar' such as harvest or Valentine's Day when the Church can celebrate aspects of the life God has given us. These are occasions of real opportunity for the Church to help people make spiritual connections with concerns that are close to their hearts. When the Church helps to forge these connections the gospel comes to life and Christ's work is done.

And day after day the pulse of life also continues in the church's own gatherings. Home groups and prayer meetings, fellowships and guilds draw many Christian people and friends together. They are places of prayer, worship, testimony and learning. Worship in these gatherings can be reluctant or stale, or it can be lively and connect the gospel to the nitty-gritty of life.

New Patterns for Worship and A Service of the Word are invaluable tools in giving shape and content to worship at all these times.

A bit of an occasion

Countless things that come up in the life of a local community make people want to gather for worship in church or even in a marquee at the park:

- formal civic occasions such as 'Mayor Making', commemorations and significant landmarks such as the completion of a phase of regeneration;

- the start and end of secular cycles such as the school year or, in commercial centres, the business year;

- summer festivals;

- anniversaries such as celebrating fifty years of a local British Legion branch;

- tragedy (see especially *New Patterns* sample service 18, Facing Pain: a Service of Lament).

When people gather specifically for worship outside the regular Sunday gatherings of the Church, many of the rules that normally dictate what should happen evaporate. This can leave those responsible for planning the occasion either gloriously free to let their imagination loose or wandering in a shapeless void, a wilderness in which there are no familiar features to help navigation. It may be different for members of the congregation, who may have fairly definite expectations – good and bad. For those being dragged along under sufferance, these expectations can be so low that even St Dodo's will exceed them. Others may have been anticipating the occasion for years and praying that it will be the harbinger of the Kingdom, yet feel let down when it is finally all over. People can have a complexity of expectations for events that don't have a regular rhythm, which can make the job of planning all the harder.

There are, of course, many places to which you can turn for help. Amongst the official provision of the Church of England, A Service of the Word and *New Patterns for Worship* will probably be most useful. Their links with the Church's tradition and the innovation they encourage strike a good balance between, on the one hand, prescriptive orders and, on the other, an anything-goes approach. This is helpful both to worship planners and congregations.

The Church at its national, diocesan and local levels also provides many opportunities for its members to gather for worship beyond Sunday parish settings. The resources in *New Patterns* also serve well as the first port of call in planning such events as deanery or diocesan worship. Road shows, conferences and meetings throughout the Church are moments that present really good opportunities for people to bring specific concerns into the arena of the Spirit. If you get involved in this sort of work, you will probably be regarded as an expert either in the subject involved or in imaginative worship. These can be really creative occasions which give you the opportunity to collaborate with a group beyond your usual immediate circle. They provide fertile ground in which new ideas can germinate, and an opportunity for wide dissemination. The Church can sometimes be quite a critical and daunting body in which you may be reluctant to take risks. ASOTW and *New Patterns* provide much wisdom and a good foundation on which to build your innovative ventures and they will help you avoid numerous pitfalls. You can use them, not to limit what is done, but as a launch pad from which to strike out in new directions.

Although *New Patterns for Worship* is probably the primary Church of England handbook for those involved in arranging worship for special occasions, it contains no specific sample services as starting points. In a sense, any of the Church's standard forms of service or any of the sample services could be used as a starting point. Hopefully the planning notes in *New Patterns* and the following chapters in this book will help you to unpack the nature of a special occasion and discover the ways in which worship might connect with it.

Some hazards of special services

Week after week churches up and down Britain organize their worship with very little fuss over logistics and practicalities. But the day the bishop visits it will all go wrong. Why?

As soon as you push the boat out, or as soon as you change the pace and rhythm of things, people can lose their footing. Church-welcomers and churchwardens, who may be in church an hour before a Sunday morning service, might only turn up straight from work for a midweek evening celebration with no time to do anything before the service starts. And the person who always lights the candles may not come at all. When you are organizing something quite different from the usual pattern, make sure you consider every detail, even those you can normally take for granted. Here are some common pitfalls to watch out for:

- If you have invited special guests or civic dignitaries, make sure that there are people in the church who know who is coming and the seating arrangements. If they are likely to bring a partner (or in some cases a driver), make good provision for them as well.

- Make sure that everybody taking a lead in the worship (including the musicians) is properly briefed. If leaders need special texts and prayers make sure they are to hand but try to avoid too many books. *New Patterns* sample service 23, All Creation Worships, demonstrates a helpful way of printing orders of service, with the full text for all the leaders and a simpler and more appropriate congregational text for everybody else.

- Don't assume that the whole congregation will be familiar with your usual practices. Some may be worshipping for the first time, so help them to follow what is happening and to feel at home.

- People who take responsibility for organization on a Sunday may not assume the responsibility naturally on a Wednesday. Check that somebody will sort out microphones, silverware, etc.

- If people are taking a lead in the worship for the first time, make sure they have a rehearsal, especially when microphones are being used.

- When you are being creative in your use of the worship space and have moved the furniture around, make sure that things are not where, for instance, an acolyte might trip over them. More importantly, make sure the building remains friendly to people with disabilities, especially if they are likely to be caught up in a crowd.

- You may need to plan how furniture and microphones are to be used.

- If the service is eucharistic, be generous in your estimation of the amount of bread and wine you will need. If the numbers are expected to be large you may also need to make provision for more places than normal at which people can receive communion. Try to provide enough books and service sheets for the number of people likely to be present.

- If you normally pass round collection plates in church, make sure you plan properly for a special service. If there is to be no collection you may need to inform people. It is not uncommon to see churchwardens hastily organizing a collection during a final hymn and arriving with it at the altar after the choir and clergy have processed out.

And when you are organizing worship in a building with which you are unfamiliar:

- It is often easier to see how you could use an unfamiliar worship space creatively but make sure you ask the owner before you push the altar to the middle or hang banners on the walls.

- Work out carefully where those who are leading worship and music should stand and brief them.

- Check you know how to use the sound system and work out any special characteristics it has.

- Don't assume that everything you use in your home church will be present elsewhere.

- If the service is eucharistic, think carefully about how people should receive. Remember that the building will also be unfamiliar to the congregation and that you will need to be able to brief them simply and clearly.

Following a 'secular calendar'

The shape of the English year and the pattern of the Church's religious calendar have impacted on each other quite strongly over a period of centuries. For most of the time they seem to be in step with each other. In what some people describe as a post-modern age, this is beginning to break down; indeed the whole

notion of a shared calendar has begun to break down. The
semester system in schools and colleges means that there is no
longer a single academic calendar and in some places Christmas
and Easter are incidental. Sunday working is a fact of life for
many people, changing the characteristics that used to shape the
week. Late night opening, shift work and the need for some
people to be permanently on-call even breaks down whatever
shared assumptions there may once have been about the shape of
a day. This all poses a set of challenges and opportunities to the
Church, many of which are outside the scope of this book. But
there are ways in which ASOTW can be used to make strong
connections with emerging features of these new calendars.

New Patterns for Worship offers ten sample services under
the heading of 'Special Days and Themes from the Secular
Calendar'. Placing the service outline for a home group meeting
and an intercessory prayer meeting under this heading is
perhaps a little dubious. The other eight are examples showing
where some connections might be found. They don't represent
out-and-out secular occasions, but seek to link the concerns of
the Christian faith community with priorities that are widely
shared in this age.

- **A Service for St Valentine's Day (Sample Service 13)**: the
  sample service makes connections between the nature of God's
  love for his people and the human love that a couple can share.
  This sort of service could be used to invite couples recently
  married in the church (and perhaps not so recently married) to
  come back. Many couples are much more open to reflecting on
  their relationship at this point of the year than at other
  times. The concept of love expressed in the CW Marriage
  Service, where human love is a grace that helps us understand
  God, is turned on its head in this St Valentine's Day sample
  service. Here God's love is used as a model that, in turn, gives
  us a greater understanding of human love.

- **A Service of the Word for Mothering Sunday (14)**: here the
  focus is on the mothers and motherly figures who surround the
  congregation and are a part of the congregation. The service
  makes strong connections between the love of God and a
  mother's love. The Song of St Anselm (over page) is a clear-cut
  example of how the spiritual traditions of the Church can

illumine today's concerns. This could be the sort of service to which you specifically invite back those who have brought children for baptism in the church over the past year.

A Song of St Anselm

1 Jesus, like a mother you gather your people to you;
   you are gentle with us as a mother with her children.

2 Often you weep over our sins and our pride,
   tenderly you draw us from hatred and judgement.

3 You comfort us in sorrow and bind up our wounds,
   in sickness you nurse us and with pure milk you feed us.

4 Jesus, by your dying, we are born to new life;
   by your anguish and labour we come forth in joy.

5 Despair turns to hope through your sweet goodness;
   through your gentleness, we find comfort in fear.

6 Your warmth gives life to the dead,
   your touch makes sinners righteous.

7 Lord Jesus, in your mercy heal us;
   in your love and tenderness remake us.

8 In your compassion bring grace and forgiveness,
   for the beauty of heaven may your love prepare us.

New Patterns for Worship, Sample Service 14

- **A Service of the Word for Fathers' Day (15):** this service focuses on what it means to have the responsibility of children and reflects this back as an example of God's care for creation. Amongst its many suggestions for achieving this is the idea that members of the congregation could publicly share experiences of fatherhood from different perspectives, concluded by a creed. The creed would, of course, begin with a statement of belief in God as Father.

Sharing experiences

The chance to let members of the congregation speak of their experiences and their faith can be an excellent way of connecting the worship to the rest of life, and can especially help visitors to see how our faith is worked out in practice. Before the sermon (or as part of it) it might be possible and appropriate to include such an element of 'testimony'. This might include, for instance:

- asking a new dad to describe the difference being a father has made to his life and his faith;

- inviting someone to share (sensitively) their experience of having a father who let them down badly, and the difference that knowing God's love has made to them;

- inviting a grandfather to speak about what it is like to be a grandparent, including any advice he has for new parents, or any things he wishes he had done differently when his children were young.

- It might be particularly appropriate to conclude such sharing with the Affirmation of Faith.

New Patterns for Worship, Sample Service 15

- **Harvest (16):** this is a very simple outline for a season in which there is a long tradition of connecting worship with the cycle of the year. The sample breaks from more traditional structures of service and uses the sermon as a commentary that can run through the liturgy.

- **A Celebration of St Luke (17):** most saints lived human lives and there are often deep resonances between their lives and people's experience of life today. This sample service aims to model a way of building on some of those resonances in worship. St Luke is chosen as a saint whose commemoration day is still often marked in the modern health industry as a day to consider the nature of the medical profession and the dedication of its workers. It is a timely occasion for the Church to celebrate the healing ministry

- **A Service of Lament (18)**: this is the sort of service that might be used in the immediate aftermath of a tragedy in which there has been loss of life. At such times there is often very little time to prepare. It could also be used for some years after such an incident as an annual act of remembrance. In Liverpool, fifteen years on, there is still pressure for a religious service each year on the anniversary of the Hillsborough disaster. However, it can sometimes be difficult to know at what point healing is best promoted by ceasing to hold great public acts of remembrance.

- Sample services **19** and **20** offer orders for a penitential rite (which could be used in Advent and Lent) and an alternative healing service to those in *Common Worship: Pastoral Services*. As such they don't fit in with a 'secular calendar' but they undoubtedly pick up on issues that people today find particularly difficult to handle.

These sample services model some of the ways that the worship of the Church might connect with the 'secular calendar' and the spirit of the age. There are other ways that are going to demand a great deal of flexibility from the Church. For instance, in many Roman Catholic churches the best attended worship of the week is the Saturday evening mass. The pattern of most church members being able to set Sunday aside as a day for worship may no longer be achievable. And the connections that those outside the Church can make with Sunday worship may also be limited because the secular calendar and the Church calendar don't overlap as they once did. The Church is free to complain about the changing priorities that determine people's routines but it must also adapt itself to these changes. The thinking that this collection of Sample Services draws together is a step along the road.

Commemoration of the faithful departed according to the 'secular' or 'religious' calendar – an alternative.

Services for the Commemoration of the Faithful Departed fit very well into the religious calendar at All Saints' tide. This is the beginning of the Church's anticipation of heaven as Advent approaches. It is the time of year when the nation remembers those who have died in war. But in the 'secular' calendar this is simply the middle of autumn, half way to Christmas after the summer.

Services of Commemoration may also appropriately take place just after Christmas. This would be out of kilter with the Church's calendar. But such a service would come at the point in the year when the recently departed will have been very deeply missed and near to the turning of the year, a time of looking forward, of hope and commitment to the future.

Small groups and worship

ASOTW can be equally useful for the regular worship that church members expect throughout the week. The problems of organizing worship for a Bible study group or a women's fellowship can be very similar to other mid-week services. This is compounded by the fact that preparation is needed time and time again. How often is worship in a Bible study group reduced to ten minutes' 'open prayer' ending up with the Grace? And how often does an afternoon fellowship meeting include worship still rooted in pre-war utilitarianism – worship that is no more than: welcome – hymn – opening prayer – Bible reading – hymn – two more prayers and the Lord's Prayer – hymn – speaker – hymn – tea and biscuits?

Now it would be possible within the strict limits of the law to still call the second of these a Service of the Word. And, of course, whether or not it either actually complies with the law is irrelevant. The Church has never attempted to legislate for such occasions, nor should it. But what are of real value, and what ASOTW and *New Patterns* do offer, are resources, ideas and models of good practice. These can help people draw more deeply from the spiritual wells of the Church than they often do. To both the study group and the fellowship meeting, these new tools of the Church can re-introduce many forgotten lessons, including:

- that attention should be paid to the gathering and the dismissal;

- that penitence is an appropriate element of worship;

- that credal statements can focus the gospel in worship;

- that Psalms and scriptural songs can help to provide deep roots for today's worshipping communities.

New Patterns may well be just the sort of resource that can bring worship back to life in the small fellowship and study groups that are dotted around the Church. In most places those responsible for Sunday worship have not had the means to organize the worship of every other church gathering and small group. Here is a self-contained volume with guidelines for planning worship, helpful commentary, samples and a smorgasbord of texts to try out. For many people who help to lead in the midweek gatherings of the Church, it may fill a gap and help them develop what they do. In some churches it might be worth formally introducing *New Patterns* to such leaders and offering them a short course to explore how they could benefit from using it.

Home groups have sprung up in many churches as echoes of the very earliest Christian communities that met in people's homes. There is much evidence that such meetings were not just occasions for conversation, but were for encouragement through worship, song and prayer. Some people today find this difficult. Two of the Sample Services offered in *New Patterns* are designed as starting points for just this sort of need. They put prayer and study where they most naturally belong, in a worship context.

- **Worship in a Small Group or an Intercessory Prayer Meeting (Sample Service 21)** is an outline that can be used to give shape to a variety of forms of home group and Bible study meetings. Often it is the case that these meetings are shaped by the logistics of hospitality and the question of when people would like a cup of tea. This outline suggests making space before reading the Bible and afterwards for discussion and study. Its shape makes space for gathering and dismissal, praise, thanksgiving, reflection on scripture and prayer. Amongst its suggestions is the idea that people could share the Peace or say the Nunc Dimittis before they leave.

This is only an idea and does not claim to be the last word. But it does demonstrate how meetings shaped by worship may be given a different texture from the business meetings that often dominate church life and may provide deep spiritual benefit to those who attend.

There are many ways outside the regular Sunday gatherings of a church in which ASOTW and *New Patterns* can make strong contributions to the Church's opportunities for drawing people into worship of God. It may be that in those churches where Sunday traditions are firmly fixed, the occasions described above will provide the only moments when ASOTW is used. In other churches such occasions will demand that ASOTW is used in a markedly different way to their normal patterns.

6 A new way of working?

The Commentary in *New Patterns for Worship* offers strong guidance on how to organize worship. It is not necessary for this to be repeated here, but there are also a host of new skills that local churches need to equip themselves with and learn to use if they are going to make the most of ASOTW. These skills are discussed below and summarized in Appendix 2.

You don't have to return to ancient history to encounter a time when clergy knew by heart all the words of all the services they were ever likely to conduct. The memory of those days still lingers. The pressure of work can considerably heighten the appeal of a liturgy which requires very little preparation. But this is a different age. Society no longer judges something as appropriate simply because it comes from an authoritative book. The approach to liturgy cultivated by the BCP will no longer stand up.

The Alternative Service Book 1980 (ASB) didn't demand very much more from ministers at the level of preparation, although it did disturb the traditional rhythm of worship. Contemporary language, a choice of eucharistic prayers, new liturgical shape and a different lectionary were among the ASB's challenges. But greater changes were under way with the emergence of 'family services' from the 1960s. These acts of worship needed real preparation and could not just be recited after cursory consideration on a Sunday morning. In some places small planning groups were established, liturgical leadership became broader based and there was a diverse use of symbols and visual aids as a focus for reflection and learning. The Alternative Worship movement of the 1980s and 90s has further extended the use of symbol, the visual, sound and smell into a new dimension and made worship accessible to a new age group. This greatly raises people's expectations for worship.

Even for those who rely on the official liturgy books of the Church, it is no longer considered possible to offer good leadership in worship without real preparation. We have high expectations of musical input, symbols, visuals, drama, dance, the shape of the liturgy and its connections to the here and now. Whilst it may not represent best practice, it may just be possible to limit the preparation of a eucharist or a funeral service to scribbling some sermon notes and making sure that the service book ribbons are in the right pages for alternative sentences, collects and seasonal material. But this simply cannot be done with ASOTW. For instance, there is no pre-printed service book to put into people's hands as they arrive. Work is involved simply to enable the congregation to follow and make their contribution to the worship, whether it is producing service cards, projection onto a screen or the careful use of remembered prayers and taught responses.

To use ASOTW well, to carry people along both in planning and worship, to be sensitive to God's beckoning and to connect with your context – all these require a wide gamut of new skills. These skills have had their place before in very specialized parts of the Church's life, but only now are they essential in almost every parish at one time or another.

Visual literacy

How words and images are presented to people, whether on a screen or by print, speaks volumes. Every style communicates something. To some extent each of us reads these implicit messages partly subliminally and partly consciously. It is important that those who send the messages know what they're saying. This is not a precise science but an art. Nevertheless, there are things that can be learnt. (Note that in the information that follows, the term 'service card' can cover a number of different formats.)

Service card tips

- Properly structured titles and subtitles, white space and ornamentation are all important cues to help people follow the service. Give some thought to them.

- Underlinings and hyphenation don't normally work well for service cards.

- Be careful where you put line breaks and page breaks, especially in congregational texts; these can act as cues for people to take a breath or pause.

- Not everybody's eyesight is the same as your own. Keep your print above 9pt and congregational texts preferably at 10pt. Coloured backgrounds lower the contrast and mean a larger typeface may be needed. Consider having a few cards printed double-size for those whose eyesight is weak.

- For children's services remember that the young don't recognize the shape a as well as they do the shape **a**. Choose your typefaces carefully.

- Pictures help. Do yours?

- Paste-ups of photocopies from various sources can look as though they were put together in a rush and so communicate that the worship is a low priority. Cards that are put together well and look attractive can help lift people's spirits.

- Ask somebody else to proof read whatever you produce; you will be blind to your own mistakes.

- Remember the copyright notices. For CW material see *A Brief Guide to Liturgical Copyright*, available from Church House Bookshop.

For a strong practical guide to all the issues around the regular and occasional production of local orders of service, see *Producing Your Own Orders of Service*, by Mark Earey (CHP/*Praxis*, 2000).

There are a wide variety of options for presenting those words of the liturgy that the congregation needs to have set before it. Each of them needs careful consideration.

- Hymn and song books carry a host of hidden messages. They are not just functional; how they look and feel carries associations for people.

- Hymn books are often used along with other media. Try to make sure that people are not overloaded with having to use a fistful of books and papers. Use of only one hymn or song book is recommended. It is as important to look organized as it is to be organized. If music from a variety of sources must be used, either print everything out or project words that are not otherwise readily to hand.

- Commercially produced service books identify the local worship strongly with a particular source and ethos; the Common Worship books form a strong identity with the Church of England. Visually such books conform to an agreed house style. Where this is strong (as it is with CW) it can be mimicked to some extent in local productions (see below).

- Service sheets and cards range from disposable photocopies to semi-permanent and hardwearing cards. By their nature they can be tailored to suit the needs of a local community better than any book. However they are produced, they are likely to be a significant focus for people during their worship. So they need to be produced with some care. Their effect is not just functional, to place the printed words under people's noses. Following a style such as CW can create a feeling of identity with the Church of England and strengthen the sense of belonging to it. This can be done through devices as simple as using the 'Ce' logo and the ¶ symbol for main headings, following the typeface choices, using subheadings near the right margin, applying the colour red, bold, italics, etc. and line spacing variations.

- OHP and computer projection: presentational software such as Microsoft PowerPoint® or AppleWorks® has greatly simplified the production of high-quality slides for the projection of words and images. The increasing accessibility of computer display projectors has made it more feasible to have a freshly created set of slides each Sunday without eating through expensive consumables such as ink and acetates (although projector bulbs can be an expensive item). Computer display projectors also facilitate smooth transitions between slides and allow moving images and perpetually animated backgrounds. For instance, an animated candle flame as a consistent feature across all the slides used for an Easter liturgy can be very effective. Or try a permanently rippling watery background for a baptismal liturgy. Simply paste a two- or three-second movie that you can make yourself into the master page of a presentation package and set it to play repeatedly.

Of course, it is easy to get carried away with the technological possibilities and lose the coherence of an act of worship in the amazement of a fantastic display. Try to use only what will contribute to people moving into a deeper encounter with God. When using a computer display projector it is important to pay attention to the readability of words more than any other presentational option. Characters need to be large and bold enough to be read at the back of the worship area and with high enough contrast from the background to be read in daylight by people with average sight. You may also need supplementary service sheets for those with poor sight. The time investment in this sort of work can be huge.

Managing the workflow

Many clergy and worship leaders may turn to ASOTW only for occasional use. If you begin to turn to it on a fairly regular basis, there are a number of other issues that you will need to bear in mind both for your own sanity and that of the congregation. This is especially relevant where bespoke worship cards or projector slides are expected.

The possibilities opened up by the freedom of ASOTW, along with desktop publishing and desktop presentational technologies, are endless. You could do something brand new each week. But if you try this, you may find that you have no time for anything else and the congregations may find themselves baffled. Certainly congregations can miss out on the benefits of texts that are familiar and memorable, such as are found in the more standard liturgies.

A second issue for worship leaders who use ASOTW and desktop publishing or presentational tools in highly flexible ways is the 'ownership' of the worship. Without real care and consultation worship can become individual and idiosyncratic, disconnected from the practice of the wider Church and leaving members of a local congregation feeling that it doesn't belong to them either. Good collaborative practice and real consultation are essential to avoid this. Letting people have a say isn't impossible. Small groups can quite easily work collectively putting together the liturgy for a service. Much larger groups can evaluate services. Talking about the worship of the past few months at regular Worship Committee meetings or annually at the PCC can be of value both to creators and consumers.

Below are some indications of how to make the best use of today's resources without becoming overburdened, confusing or remote:

- All of the liturgical resources and flexible structures that are emerging give some real encouragement for a fresh approach to worship. But don't try to create a fresh new service from top to bottom every week. The congregation will find it confusing and you will have no time to do anything else. The Church of England's seasonal provision is rooted in a long history with deep resonances drawing on salvation history. You can allow this to dictate the pace of change for many aspects of the liturgy. Apart from occasional feast days there are only nine major season changes in the year.

- Having settled on the broad framework for a season you can still introduce change without rewriting everything. Distinguish in your printing or slides between those things which will run from week to week and those which are for the day. People will always expect the hymns and readings to change and regulars will find it easy to dip into separate books to follow them. In Communion services the Eucharistic Prayers could also change day by day, or the Psalms and Canticles in a simple service of Morning Prayer. By preparing them separately from the core material, you can cut your own workload down and retain some elements that regulars will clearly recognize as having some continuity. (There is further discussion of this in *Liturgy and Technology*, by Tim Stratford (Grove Worship Series 154, Grove Books, 1999).)

- Don't feel that everything that can be different from week to week should be. Try running intercessions of the same form over a season. (This is even possible with collects: the old pattern of a single Lenten or Advent collect could replace the weekly ones.) The use of a semi-familiar response and prayer between biddings that are concerned with the here and now can be helpful. (For discussion about this see Anna de Lange and Liz Simpson's helpful training manual, *Leading Intercessions* (Grove Worship Series 169, Grove Books, 2002).)

- Pictures speak louder than words. A few carefully chosen illustrations that help direct thoughts towards the focus of the worship and that become familiar can serve well.

- Using a slow cycle of change gives opportunity for discussion of service outlines beforehand and evaluation of worship afterwards by congregational members and worship committees. It also leaves the door open to develop collaborative practices for the drafting of material.

Sensitivity to God and the context of worship

Centrally produced liturgies have the advantage that there is little expectation of them directly addressing particular local needs.

Those responsible for organizing the service choose hymns, prayers and perhaps readings that speak to the context, but other poetic resonances are picked up through personal sensitivity, chance, and the coincidences that are evidence of the consistency of God's ways both today and in history. ASOTW changes both the expectations and the reality. Given all its flexibility, the role of the worship leader becomes that of a guide who offers people many explicit and intended points of connection with those things that bring them together in worship. This is true for Sunday-by-Sunday worship and even more true when worship is occasioned by a particular missionary or pastoral context.

A host of skills that shouldn't be undervalued are demanded here. These include:

- Sensitivity to other people (being able to read a variety of contexts and gain some understanding of the agendas that people are likely to bring with them to worship). Prayerfulness in preparation and sensitivity to God's leading.

- The ability to share the creative process with others. Such collaboration involves being both assertive enough to make a contribution and humble enough to let go of personal hobbyhorses. It also helps if those who take the strongest lead are sensitive to the dynamics of group work.

- The ability to make connections between the Bible, the traditions of the Church and the pastoral needs of those gathering for worship.

Those who have trained for ordination and other formal ministries may have had the opportunity to address these issues, but this may not be so for every church member who finds themselves working with ASOTW. Such training opportunities may need to be offered locally. (Appendix 2 offers a summary of the issues raised in this chapter that could form part of a curriculum for liturgical education and training in the use of A Service of the Word.) In a more immediate and practical way, the Guidelines for worship provided in *New Patterns for Worship* (p. 20) and reprinted in the panel on the following page can be used as a checklist for reviewing what is done.

A checklist for worship

- Is there a balance between word, prayer, praise and action? For instance the Word section may be top heavy with long readings and long introductions, or too many short readings.

- Is the worship directed to God, addressing him rather than the people?

- Is the structure and direction of the service clear enough for people to know where it is going? Does the service have an overall coherence, or is it just one item after another?

- When is the climax to the service? If there is more than one, is that deliberate? Is the emotional or spiritual climax the same as the climactic moment in terms of music or words or congregational action? There is no 'right' answer, but it helps if service planners are aware of these ways in which the service develops.

- What space is there for reflection or silence in the service?

- How much of the service might be classed as 'entertainment'? Is this justified? Is there a balance between receiving (listening, watching, contemplating) and responding? Check on posture: is there too much sitting down or standing up at one time? Or, conversely, are people bobbing up and down too much? Is there enough action?

- Is the music used in such a way as to further and develop the main thrust of the service? Is there too much musical praise, with too many choir items, or too long a section of choruses from the music group, or hymns too close to one another?

- Does the form of service enable the gifts of a variety of people in the church to be used in both planning and taking part?

- Compare this service with other services in the month. An occasional completely new form of worship may stimulate people to discover new dimensions to their ordinary worship, but a new pattern each week may be confusing and unsettling, particularly to children. If people are familiar with both structure and content of the service, they feel more secure and can take part more easily. For an all age service, for instance, it may be better to have a standard structure, with 'windows' or 'slots' which can be changed from week to week.

- Especially if you are planning 'family worship', check that the contents do not exclude some in the congregation, e.g. children, single people, the bereaved, members of broken families. It is hurtful and not constructive to require a mixed congregation simply to join in prayers thanking God for our homes and families and all the happiness that parents and children share.

Drama, ceremonial and movement

ASOTW positively encourages innovation in the development of ceremonial and the use of symbol. There are many ways in which movement, drama and everyday objects can be used to lead people on in their worship of God. Whilst much of this can be achieved within the normally recognized conventions, skills and practices already to be found in churches, there is a great deal more to be learnt from other disciplines.

- Voice production, imaginative speaking techniques, story telling and microphone use are all learnt skills that don't necessarily come naturally. There can be a marked difference between a polished actor reading a passage like John 1 and the way this is read in many parish churches. Churches could consider offering some training to those who contribute the spoken word to their worship. Make use of professional help: there may be a local actor or drama society that could offer a session on speaking with a smile or gravitas, pacing it right and keeping it colourful. Where the key issue is that of basic adult literacy, look to the local FE college. They will often be prepared to run an appropriate course on your premises and may even pay you rent! If these things are not viable for the local church alone, why not do it across the deanery?

- It is important for the minister or president to know their place or role. They will rarely have responsibility for doing everything but will often have the key responsibility for holding the shape and order of a service together. This can be done like the conductor of an orchestra, with very little intrusion, or it can be done like the principal player in a pantomime, who maintains a high degree of interaction. Both styles have their place, but also their appropriate times. How the president or ministers are going to handle things and the skills of the people concerned need thinking through. Sometimes this thinking may need to go beyond your usual ideas.

Some worship may be bold and brash, bringing home clear lessons of salvation history; alternatively, it may be poetic and aesthetic, attempting to create awareness of God through the numinous. Either way ASOTW can be used as the liturgical framework. Right from the beginning, when you decide on how the service is to be ordered, through to the leadership of the service itself, you will need to be sensitive to the movement of the worship. *New Patterns* contains a resource section about action and movement in worship, though much of the focus there is on the action of distributing and receiving communion. There is also some good advice about symbol and ceremonial. *New Patterns* distinguishes three types of symbol:

- symbols which people bring with them (e.g. everybody dressing in red on Pentecost Sunday);

- symbols and actions which are individual (such as genuflecting);

- symbols and actions uniting the congregation (such as sharing the Peace).

The panel opposite develops this third type of symbol.

Examples of contemporary symbols

- Light: A candle isn't the only symbol of light that can be used in worship. Oil lamps are perhaps more biblical and in today's contexts can be represented by using anything from a Victorian table light to some very modern creations. Torches and spotlights can also be used to great effect.

- Fire: Be careful indoors! Equipment able to create large realistic flames by airflow, fabric and a light (such as 'Le Flame') is available from theatrical equipment suppliers or hire shops. This can produce a truly dramatic effect, say for Pentecost, without the insurance risks that would come with a real flame.

- Colour: You can use the four traditional colours of the Church in much more dramatic ways than simple altar frontals and vestments. Large bright flags made of lightweight material fixed onto garden canes can be waved in songs and hymns by dancers (and children) to great effect. These banners can be used to represent joy (reds and oranges), herald the King of Kings (purples and whites) or the victory of good over evil (bright and sombre colours in combination).

- The carpenter's son: On occasions when people's work is the focus of their gathering in church, the tools of their trade can be carried to the altar and symbolically offered to God. This is familiar in many rural settings with the tools and fruits of farming. Firefighters, police, health service workers, those involved in education, shop workers, those in manufacturing, etc., are all able to find symbols of their work that resonate with the gospel of Jesus the friend of fishermen, the healer and teacher. Everyday things for those who attend, such as a firefighter's breathing set, a police radio, or a loaf of bread, can represent strong connections with the gospel of life, hope and love.

Collaboration

To some ears the word 'collaboration' may sound secretive and associated with the Vichy Regime of 1940s France. Here it is intended to convey the kind of leadership that has moved beyond cooperation to the actual delivery of work by a group. It is not about a group of lay people doing the vicar's 'dirty work' or simply pulling in the same direction as the vicar, but about a group taking on joint responsibility for something.

If ASOTW is to be used well, some form of collaborative working is essential. It is unlikely that one person will have all the skills required. The priest who is musically sensitive, IT aware, theatrically trained, locally bred, a professional seamstress, child friendly and disability conscious is rare. The fixed liturgies of the Church have themselves emerged from a complicated collaborative process which takes many perspectives into account. ASOTW makes all of this the responsibility of local leaders. Those who take it on should open their eyes to some possibilities which may be new to them.

- The clergy aren't right about everything. They can offer to the worship enterprise distinctive skills and formational background. This may mean becoming a resource rather than the sole decision-maker.

- Collaboration requires organization. If the worship diary isn't managed and forward planning doesn't happen, people won't know where they are or how they can contribute.

- Groups that are going to collaborate need to give some time to understanding themselves. Exercises in group dynamics and a programme of liturgical education are both important for worship planners. It is as important for groups to be able to release the reluctant contributor as it is to manage their leadership and this will mean some openness about the particular personalities that make up the group.

- ASOTW offers people a new relationship to a liturgy that is no longer dropped down from above in a one-size-fits-all format. Local worship planners also need to ensure that they don't try to impose their own preferences and peccadilloes on it.

- There may be local skills in the church or parish community that have gone unnoticed. Look for them and use them.

Engaging with the Word

Whatever symbols, drama, action, music or images are used in ASOTW it is the Word of God that should remain central. Other than the Preparation and the Conclusion, the service comprises only the Liturgy of the Word and Prayers. Everything about this provision serves to help people engage with God's Word and respond to it. But remember that the Word of God is both written in the pages of the Bible and living.

The authorized service outline for ASOTW, when it doesn't form part of a Communion, is more specific in what it says the Liturgy of the Word includes.

- readings (or a reading) from Holy Scripture

- a psalm, or, if occasion demands, a scriptural song

- a sermon

- an authorized Creed, or, if occasion demands, an authorized Affirmation of Faith.

New Patterns for Worship, page 11

The notes on the content of the Liturgy of the Word for the non-eucharistic service encourage the following provision:

- there should be at least two readings from the Bible, which should come from an authorized lectionary during the times of the year when the seasonal aspect is strong (Advent 3 to Epiphany 1 and Palm Sunday to Trinity Sunday);

- the word 'sermon' is only used as shorthand for a diverse approach that includes 'less formal exposition of the scriptures, the use of drama, interviews, discussion, audio-visuals' etc.

- the Liturgy of the Word doesn't have to follow any set order (only the basic ingredients are defined) and it may be that parts of it are repeated – for example, a reading could be split into three sections each followed by a song and some dialogue.

The Sermon

In ASOTW preparing a sermon begins to mean something quite different from what has come to be expected in the Church of England. Some new thinking about the nature and purpose of a sermon is needed both by those who preach them and those who receive them.

The sermon is the place where the Scriptures are opened up and provide light for reflection on the Word of God as it speaks to the here and now. That can mean several things:

- Teaching: this understanding of the sermon's purpose dominates much preaching. Teaching can be expository and historical or ethical and applied to contemporary life. Here the preacher communicates through his or her own insights and learning drawn from experience and study. This approach makes heavy demands on the preacher's personal resources. The tools of the trade include commentaries, parabolic stories, humour, poetic resonance and sometimes visual aids. Some of the most powerful and erudite preachers use this style most heavily, but it is not the only possible model and in much worship is not necessarily the most appropriate.

- Re-telling: it is often possible to translate the stories of the Bible into a context closer to today's so that the Word of God can be better understood. Here drama and story-telling are key skills. Such story-telling can often have an underlying philosophy that is very much akin to the teaching approach – the preacher has the message and uses story or drama as a tool to get his or her message across. Alternatively, the stories of Scripture can be told straight and allowed to communicate for themselves; for instance, it is a common practice to read one of the Passion Narratives from start to finish on Palm Sunday.

Old Testament stories such as Jonah and Ruth can also be used in this way.

- Testimony: it may be that someone has experienced God's hand in their lives in a way that parallels the events and experiences of Scripture. The traditional understandings of preaching can pressurize preachers into concocting a story. Looking beyond their own personal imagination to the experience of others and giving them a voice can be liberating and make the sermon come alive. Interview techniques and an awareness of what God is doing among local people are keys to this.

- Closed questions: it often helps people, especially children, to keep focused on something when they are drawn into it. Closed questions are those where the questioner knows the answer. Activities, quizzes and questions with prizes, all firmly under the control of the preacher, are means of retaining attention and achieving some level of teaching. Scattering prizes such as wrapped sweets will ensure a high level of participation for children – and often for adults too.

- Open question dialogues: the preacher often doesn't have all the answers, especially where people's lives are shaped by a different culture from his or her own. Few preachers have the personal resources to offer three or four teaching sermons a week that are worth listening to. Opening the Bible enough for local people to carry on reflecting on the parallels between the experiences of Scripture and their own, followed again by space in which they can share their insights with each other, is an emerging technique in Urban Priority Areas and may be appropriate elsewhere. It taps a resource of faithful response to God's Word which extends beyond the minister and may have a relevance to many worshippers that is all the greater because the contributors can speak of what has been lived out locally.

- Journeys of the spirit and imagination, meditative techniques, and styles borrowed from Ignatian practices can work well with groups of adults. They encourage people to put themselves prayerfully into the story and feel the impact of the Scriptures on themselves. Such a use of the sermon slot may include much silence for reflection as well as the talk itself.

Open seasons and closed seasons

Common Worship offers strong encouragement to use an authorized lectionary (backed up by legislation!). This doesn't affect occasional midweek services but it does impact on regular Sunday worship, where there is a choice of only two lectionaries: *The Book of Common Prayer* Lectionary and the *Common Worship* Lectionary (which for the Principal Sunday Service is broadly the same as the ecumenical *Revised Common Lectionary*).

The BCP Lectionary offers a table of readings for Morning and Evening Prayer. Its Holy Communion Lectionary offers a Collect, an Epistle and a Gospel reading for each Sunday of the year. A set of additional collects, an Old Testament reading and a Psalm are now available as a supplement for each Sunday.

The CW Lectionary occupies a three-year cycle and gives readings for a Principal Sunday Service and also a second and a third service. The choice of which service is which on a Sunday is left for local decision. For instance, in those churches that have an early morning Sunday Eucharist, the Principal Service will most likely be the second service of the day. For some of the year there is a choice of readings for the Principal Service, depending on whether you want to read through biblical books almost continuously week after week or want some relation between a particular Sunday's readings. Such a wide-ranging Bible reading scheme has been adopted by the Church in the hope that churches of all traditions will find it an attractive way of organizing their reading of Scripture. If this happens the Church at large may be brought more into step with itself.

There can be all sorts of reasons why from time to time it is desirable to depart from this centrally ordered scheme. These occasions when a church decides to work with ASOTW to give a particular focus to its worship are likely to be the occasions that also demand a particular choice of readings that differ from the lectionary provision. The CW lectionary allows for this by the provision of an 'open season' and a 'closed season'. During the 'closed season' the Lectionary should be followed for regular worship. During the 'open season' and for occasional services you can write your own lectionary. Bear in mind:

- The Church continues to encourage local congregations to follow the shared lectionary provision as a means of promoting a shared journey in reflection and discipleship, particularly around Christmas and Easter (always 'closed seasons') when it is unlikely anyway that there would be much value in departing from the scriptures strongly associated with those seasons.

- 'Closed seasons' are protected by Canon Law, which lays down that an authorized lectionary must be followed for a Communion Service from Advent 1 until 2 February and from Ash Wednesday until Trinity Sunday. All Saints' Day is a mini closed season all of its own.

- ASOTW without communion makes provision for even greater freedom, with only two short 'closed seasons': Advent 3 to Epiphany 1 and Palm Sunday to Trinity Sunday.

- At any other time of the year you can do your own thing, provided that you recognize that the authorized lectionaries are the norm, and that the minister consults the PCC.

This allows for locally arranged themes to be followed, for instance as part of an evangelistic or stewardship campaign. It also allows a particular book of the Bible to be studied through, for example, a series of expositions. *New Patterns for Worship* offers an excellent set of sample lectionary models for this.

Making connections

The connections which worship makes with the lives of a community outside the church can often be very tenuous. There are some traditional points of connection: sometimes the building itself makes connections with the story of a community through events, stories and people captured on stained glass, stone and brass plaques, banners and displays. The most common connections made within the words of worship are in the prayers of intercession. But these connections are often only perfunctory. The CW Holy Communion intercession structure invites prayers for

---

- The Church of Christ
- Creation, human society, the Sovereign and those in authority
- The local community
- Those who suffer
- The communion of saints.

Common Worship, page 174

Some of these are often treated minimally and only the sick and the dead are prayed for by name. The use of Sunday-by-Sunday intercession diaries, which enable prayer for the roads of a parish, other community sector allies and local service providers, electoral roll members, etc., is sadly still rare. Where such things are produced locally they make a strong contribution to worship. The use of diaries such as *The Anglican Cycle of Prayer* or diocesan prayer diaries can also help. Prayers shouldn't just repeat the previous day's news bulletins but should echo the concerns of the congregation. An awareness of the issues of national and world news that will be on people's minds should inform public intercession.

But beyond this ASOTW invites its users to create far more connections which resonate with the immediately surrounding world. In some cases this will happen because ASOTW has provided the basis for a special service. In other cases those who prepare the liturgy will need to work hard to discern the points of connection. (Some indications that might help are offered in the following panel.)

Connections beyond the Intercessions

- The intercessions are a clear and familiar way for the worshipping community to hold the wider concerns of life and the locality before God. Don't forget to pray for the hale and hearty as well as the sick and the departed. Often the 'well' are carrying big concerns and real burdens. Where personal concerns are raised in public prayer, don't forget to ask people first. The use of prayer diaries for electoral roll members, organizations, local streets, etc. can be a helpful discipline in encouraging regular prayer.

- The so-called 'sermon' slot (which may not be a sermon at all and need not be a single slot – see page 92) is a key moment when the concerns of those who have gathered can be considered in the light of God's Word. Such connections are less likely to be made by a traditional teaching model than by the use of techniques such as open question dialogues or prepared 'testimonies' which allow the concerns of the here and now to be expressed and interpreted.

- Action, drama and symbol are important ways through which contemporary concerns can be held up for reflection in the context of worship. Symbols need not be confined to the traditionally religious. At a celebration of 250 years of coal mining in a Lancashire town the work, fellowship and hope of coal miners were represented respectively by coal (a great one hundredweight chunk), an SOS name-tag and a Davy lamp. Each was offered at the altar at points in the service which were surrounded by music, readings and prayers that resonated with the symbol (ideas that the miners themselves came up with). Connecting such symbols with the word of God can be echoed in prayer, song, poetry, dance and sermon. The flexibility of structure allowed by ASOTW means that the shape of a service can be dictated by the symbols being offered or the actions done.

- The traditional liturgical material of the Church, its canticles, psalms and the writings of its 'Fathers', forms a huge corpus from which careful selection can be made to resonate with the concerns and aspirations of today. But the poetry and rhetoric of the Church extends beyond the traditional. Writing which is not intended for liturgical use, such as that of Dietrich Bohoeffer, or that which is, such as the work of the Iona Community's Wild Goose Worship Group, can make very powerful connections, especially where the context for worship is related to the context from which they were writing.

- In non-eucharistic use of ASOTW, experiment with the collects. They may only be short but they perform an important job as 'girding' prayers at transitional points of the liturgy such as when moving from 'Gathering' to 'The Word of God'. There is a general consensus that the contemporary language collects of CW bear too much relation to AD 1662 and too little to AD 2000. Locally written prayers that negotiate liturgical transitions more explicitly may often be more appropriate. Perhaps the time will come when a flexible form of collect will be permitted, on the lines of:

  'God whose nature is . . . , help us whose nature is not fully fit for heaven to hear your word, draw close to you in worship and hold our world before you in prayer . . .'

- Choose Bible readings carefully and expect other parts of the liturgy and hymnody to evoke responses and interpretation. Don't worry if they're not totally in line with each other; there is more than just one way for a mixed complex of connections to touch the rich mix of complex people that inevitably makes up a congregation. Remember that outside the principal service on a Sunday there is no requirement for you to use a particular set of lectionary readings.

A sense of mission

George Carey, when he was Archbishop of Canterbury, suggested that worship is the shop window of the Church. This idea that it is in worship that those who look can see the best of what the Church is about, neatly and succinctly set out in an ordered and attractive way, should perhaps be more true than in reality it is. But the mission of the Church must never hang entirely on worship. Without a church life actively engaging with the world beyond its walls, worship becomes empty. A Service of the Word offers both encouragement and a framework to create worship that builds on that engagement, but it can't carry the mission of the Church all on its own.

Many of the standard liturgies of the Church themselves have their roots in the Church's mission. The Eucharist clearly proclaims Christ's saving love and the Common Worship service orders offer a language that helps to maintain this in twenty-first-century Britain. ASOTW offers increased flexibility of structure and content for both eucharistic and non-eucharistic worship, allowing a greater place for concerns that are more sharply focused than they often are in regular Sunday worship. You should base worship on this provision when this is precisely what you want to do.

One pitfall to be avoided in the use of ASOTW is to make it a watered down version of the Church's real worship. This serves no one. Rich, deep, resonant, significant ways in which worship can draw people into encounter with God are always to be found. ASOTW can provide an enabling framework but it can be empty of content. So beware!

Should it be a Communion service?

This question is very sharp in a missionary context. To some people worship seems incomplete without communion. Others can feel excluded by the Church's discipline of admission to communion. The Eucharist can be a converting sacrament that invites everyone, those who feel on the edge as well as those in the middle of things, into closer fellowship with God and the Church. To some it can be an obstacle. Where ASOTW is used as a means of meeting a particular missionary focus, the place of communion needs thinking through carefully. There are a number of factors that might affect the decision:

- How many of those expected will be excluded from receiving communion and how will they interpret this? As the Church's exclusivity or as the Church offering them a challenge to move forward in their discipleship?

- If you are inviting community leaders and representatives who may not be able to receive communion in the Church of England, will this cause offence?

- Will this congregation understand what is happening in a Communion service?

- Is the service intended primarily for children? If so, where do they stand in relation to the Church's policy on admission to communion? (For more discussion of this issue see Chapter 3.)

- Are there any time constraints on the service? If there are, it may be impossible to find time to do justice to prayer, praise, reflection on God's Word, action, symbol, drama, penitence, *and* communion. Sometimes the need to be focused determines the answer.

- Is a priest going to preside?

Models for Worship and Mission

There is no definitive list of when and why ASOTW is appropriate as a tool for mission, but there are some tried and tested models for the place of worship in the mission of the Church. Much of the Church of England's provision for worship in volumes such as *Common Worship: Initiation Services* and *Common Worship: Pastoral Services* belongs to the sphere of worship and mission. What follows is a discussion of where the broader provision of ASOTW is most appropriate.

- **Seeker Services:** There can be value in designing worship for congregations of those who are seeking after faith, without being compromised by having to cater for the people who have already found their way into membership of the Church. These services shouldn't be an apology for worship in the sense that they make excuses but should be *apologia* in the sense that there is interpretation and a supportive approach that helps people find their way into the presence of God. Nor should they be all talk and presentation, but should allow space for a spiritual response. The connections that such services make with their participants may well be in the realm of the 'spirit of the age' and must extend beyond the Church's institutional concerns.

- **Sector Services:** Civic services and other occasions when community and public sector agencies gather to hold their sorrows or their celebrations before God present real opportunities in many churches for the mission of the Church to be extended into worship. The Church shouldn't shy away from the hurt and pain or the joy and celebration, but hold them before God as powerfully as possible. Look beyond the usual words into silence, symbol and action.

- **Project Services:** Many churches (in particular those in Urban Priority Areas) manage, sponsor and support a wide range of projects. Some of these can be central to the church's ministry (e.g. a youth club), some are primarily building users (e.g. a slimming club), some are neither (such as a federation of local voluntary sector groups) – but all are of real service to the local community and represent the Church's mission there. Offering them conscious opportunities to enter the presence of God and find there a greater significance in their efforts is a distinctive and important part of the relationship between the worshipping community and these other church-based projects. ASOTW is an ideal tool in the creation of such 'apt liturgies'.[1]

- **Church Parades:** Giving significance to the place of the many children's organizations that surround a church is common. Church Parade Services involving Scouts and Guides and Boys' Brigades etc. are long-standing examples. Key to an understanding of the missionary significance of these events is that they provide an opportunity to celebrate personal achievements, gifts, hopes and dreams and service rendered.

So ASOTW opens up a wide range of opportunities to the Church. It also makes new demands for increasing the skills of local worship leaders and congregations. A summary of the points made above can be found in Appendix 2. It is hoped that this could form the curriculum for a series of parish or deanery training events.

Appendix I
Some resources

Listed here are resources and publications, some of which have been referred to in the earlier chapters, related to some of the key aspects of worship we have been considering. There is a great deal of material available and this list is not intended to be exhaustive, merely illustrative.

All-age worship

Diana Murrie and Steve Pearce, *Children and Holy Communion; preparing to welcome children at Holy Communion*, National Society / Church House Publishing, 1997.

Peter Reiss, *Children and Communion*, Grove Books, 1998.

Roots Worship and *Roots Children and Young People* available from Roots Subscriptions, 4 John Wesley Rd, Peterborough, PE4 6ZP (replaces *Partners in Learning*, Methodist Church and NCEC).

SALT, Scripture Union (published quarterly).

Susan Sayers, *Living Stones*, Kevin Mayhew, Year C 1997, Year A 1998, Year B 1999.

Alternative worship

Paul Roberts, *Alternative Worship in the Church of England*, Grove Books, 1999.

Sue Wallace, *Multi-Sensory Prayer*, Scripture Union, 2000 (a resource book that moves out of the realm of texts and explores 'action').

Learning from Judaism

Michelle Guinness, *A Little Kosher Seasoning*, Hodder and Stoughton, 1994.

Valerie Irving, *Let us Keep the Feast*, Anzea, 1990 (a practical guide to the celebration of 'The New Covenant Passover').

Liturgical music (other than hymns and songs)

John L. Bell, *Come All You People*, Wild Goose Publications, 1994.

Carey Landrey, *Psalms and Songs of Faith*, North American Liturgy Resources, 1982.

Songs and Prayers from Taizé, Mowbray, 1991

Common Ground, St Andrew's Press, 1998.

Morning and Evening Prayer

A Wee Worship Book, Wild Goose Worship Resource Group (3rd edition, 2002).

Kathy Galloway (ed.), *The Pattern of Our Days*, Wild Goose Publications, 1996.

Sarah James (ed.), *The Mothers' Union Worship Book*, MU Enterprises, 1995.

Planning worship

Mark Earey, *Leading Worship*, Grove Books, 1999.

Mark Earey, *Producing Your Own Orders of Service*, Church House Publishing, 2000.

Trevor Lloyd, *A Service of the Word*, Grove Books, 1999.

Anna de Lange and Liz Simpson, *How to . . . Lead the Prayers*, Grove Books, 2002.

John Leach, *Leading Worship that Connects*, Anglican Renewal Ministries, 1999.

Songs and Prayers from Taizé, Mowbray, 1991.

New Patterns for Worship material will be available on *Visual Liturgy 4.0* in April 2003.

Small groups

Chris Bowater, *The Resource for Small Group Worship*, Kevin Mayhew, 2000–2001.

Special occasions or contexts

Ann Morisy, *Beyond the Good Samaritan*, Mowbray, 1997.

Wendy S. Robins (ed.), *Let All the World; Liturgies, litanies and prayers from around the world*, USPG, 1991.

Appendix 2
Training issues

The headings offered below are lifted out of Chapter 6 and may help to provide the core topics for a locally produced training programme to help people make better use of ASOTW. They also have a more general application to the whole sphere of developing good liturgical practice. This list was first put together at a series of workshops involving liturgical leaders from most English dioceses during the Liturgical Commission's September 2000 Consultation at the University of York.

These are skills that have always been part of the liturgical enterprise; ASOTW now expects them to be available locally.

- Sensitivity to particular contexts and agendas: the choice of particular biblical and thematic material when departing from a set lectionary; listening to God.

- Relearning God's Word: how to focus on it; preaching styles and non-didactic approaches.

- How to connect with life: testimony and intercessions, etc.

- A sense of drama: developing ceremonial; using space; using symbol beyond words; an awareness of the numinous; purposeful reflection; self-restraint.

- Practical leadership issues: multi-media; lighting techniques; stage management; voice production and imaginative speaking techniques; story-telling; conducting techniques both formal and informal.

- Facilitating collaboration: respecting the skills of others; working as a group; managing a diary and forward planning.

- Visual literacy: typography; printing and design techniques.

- Managing change: having eyes open to new possibilities;

thinking beyond received structure (including the ecumenical picture); working with each other's varied assumptions; an awareness of the needs of a congregation (including the need for people to be assertive and motivated in their interaction with change).

Notes

1 The directory approach

1. A Service of the Word has been authorized for use since 1993, was published in *Patterns for Worship* in 1995, and can also be found in *Common Worship: Services and Prayers for the Church of England*, pages 21–7.

2. This page in the *Alternative Service Book 1980* listed the themes around which the lectionary, collects, prefaces and Bible sentences were based Sunday by Sunday. To some people it was a helpful prop, for others it seemed to straitjacket and limit thinking.

3. There are copyright licensing schemes available to help handle this for you. For hymns and songs contact Christian Copyright Licensing, PO Box 1339, Eastbourne, East Sussex, BN21 1AD. Much liturgical music is also covered by Calamus, 30 North Terrace, Mildenhall, Suffolk IP28 7AB.

2 All-age worship

1. This song is often printed as a chorus only. You can find it with its verses for a cantor in *Music from Taizé Volume 1*, Collins, 1982 or *Hymns Old and New*, Kevin Mayhew, 1996.

2. E.g. A Psalm for All Seasons in *Colour the World with Song*, Carey Landrey, NALR, 1982.

3 Eucharistic all-age worship

1. Steve Pearce and Diana Murrie, *Children and Holy Communion*, CHP/National Society, 1997, pp. 4–5.

4 Morning and Evening Prayer

1. Brother Roger, in Taizé, *Songs and Prayers from Taizé*, Geoffrey Chapman, Mowbray, 1991, page 7 (reprinted by Continuum, 2002).

6 A new way of working?

1. For a discussion of this model of church and of the place of 'apt liturgies' see Ann Morisy's book, *Beyond the Good Samaritan*, Mowbray, 1997.

Index

Note: Page references in *italics* indicate grey text boxes offering tips and information; page references in **bold** type indicate extracts from *New Patterns for Worship*.